D1458526

INTERVENTION
IN RUSSIA
1918–1920

INTERVENTION
IN RUSSIA
1918–1920

A CAUTIONARY TALE

by

MILES HUDSON

LEO COOPER

First published in Great Britain in 2004 by
LEO COOPER
an imprint of Pen & Sword Books
47 Church Street,
Barnsley,
South Yorkshire,
S70 2AS

Copyright © 2004 by Miles Hudson

ISBN 1 84415 033 X

A catalogue record for this book
is available from the British Library

Typeset in 11/13pt Sabon by
Phoenix Typesetting, Burley-in-Wharfedale, West Yorkshire

Printed in England by CPI UK

To

PATRICIA

CONTENTS

LIST OF MAPS

ACKNOWLEDGMENTS

First, I would like to acknowledge the enormous contribution the Imperial War Museum has made to the research for this book. The Staff has been unfailingly helpful over many months in finding for me documents of one sort or another produced by no less than forty-eight different servicemen who 'were there' – notably A.E. Thompson, Major McPherson, Captain Wood and Engineer Rear-Admiral Shrubsole. Of the many books I have read and used, mentioned in the Bibliography, I must single out Ullman's three-volume *Intervention and the War*, a most scholarly and lucid exposition of the drama as it developed. Max Arthur's *The True Glory*, the Royal Navy 1914–39, Hodder and Stoughton, furnished me with some fascinating quotations and Rhodes' *The Anglo-American Winter War with Russia*, Greenwood Press, provided me with rare insights into the American attitude to the conflict, as did Halliday's *Ignorant Armies*, Weidenfeld and Nicolson. The Hampshire Regimental Archives, under the benevolent eye of Lt Colonel Darrock, have helped a great deal, as has Lt Colonel Fifield of the same regiment with his unrivalled knowledge of Siberia. The Bovingdon Tank Museum also has been very useful in several contexts. Henry Wilson of Pen and Sword has been most helpful and Tom Hartman's eagle eye and attention to detail have been superb.

I thank my son Mark, my great friend Sir John Stanier, and my fellow officer Bobby Collins for reading through the original manuscript and making most pertinent suggestions. I must also thank Charles Painter, Colonel Riviere, Bob Vincent and Leslie Missen for giving me interviews some twenty years ago, and my father whose journal I have read avidly and who talked to me at length about his time in Russia.

I am grateful to Dr Mary Douglas for drawing my attention to the *Punch* cartoon of 16 April 1919, which I have included in the illustrations.

The Central Asian Society journals, including lectures by Major-Generals Dunsterville and Malleson, Sir George McCartney and Captain Norris, have been most valuable.

My typist, Jenny House, has been indefatigable and cheerful throughout.

Any resemblances in this book to any persons alive or dead are entirely intentional.

Finally I must thank my wife who puts up with me.

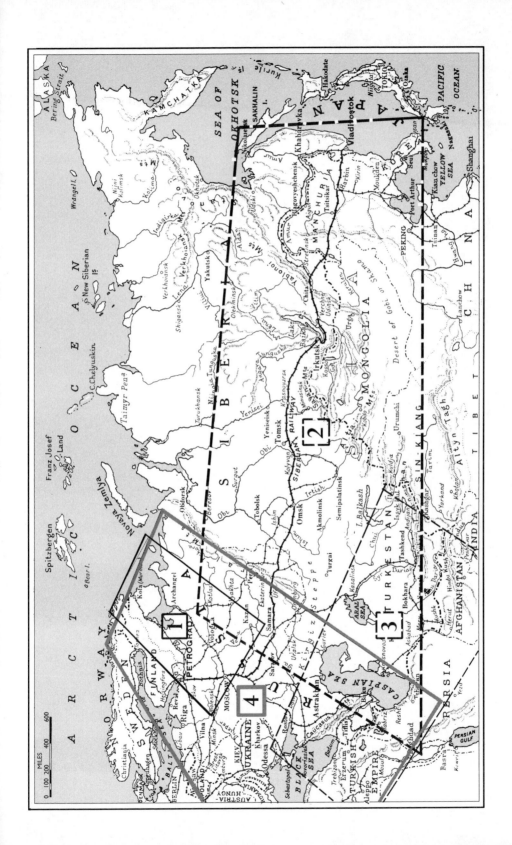

INTRODUCTION

The walking stick in the hall looked old and rather weather-beaten, more so than its companion, a more substantial specimen of utilitarian size and shape. Sheathed in tatty leather, the old one had clearly known better days. My father never seemed to use it, always choosing the other on his periodic health-giving forays. All of eight years old, I occasionally used to go with him, excited and perhaps a little apprehensive as to whether or not I would be able to keep up with what seemed to me to be his relentless march.

It had never really occurred to me to question his choice in this matter, nor indeed in anything else. To children, things are what they are. He was my hero and that was that. How could it be otherwise? Nevertheless, breaking with habit, one day I did ask him why he never took the old one – was it no good?

'It's not really a walking stick,' he replied. 'It's a swordstick.'

'What's that?' I asked.

'Well,' he said. 'Just watch.' Pulling on the handle and holding the sheath with the other hand, with a flourish he extracted a sword, thin, long and clearly dangerous. He stood there, brandishing it in triumph and began to wave it around.

I was dumbfounded. Eventually, 'What's it for?'

'Well,' he said, 'when I was in Russia and went for a walk, I never quite knew who I would meet and this might have come in useful.'

'Did you ever have to use it?'

'No. I didn't. But I might have. Things were a bit funny there at one time.'

1

'Why were you there?'

'Well, that's a long story,' he said. 'At first we were told we were guarding a million rifles at a place called Archangel in the north of Russia and after that we were fighting the Bolos.'

'Who were they?'

'The Bolsheviks.'

'Who won?'

'Well, I suppose they did. Anyway, we all had to leave in the end. A lot of people were killed.'

Thus was my interest in Russia first aroused. As I grew up, I had many talks to him about it. He never really spoke much about the First World War with its squalor and all-pervading tragedy, but Russia in 1919 was different, an exciting and, as far as he was concerned, a comparatively danger-free coda to the horrors of the trenches. He showed me the journal he had written when it was all over and the more I learned about this episode in his life and that of many others the more it fascinated me. So much so that when I had to decide what subjects I would read at Oxford when I arrived there in 1947, hot-foot from trying, with others, to keep the peace in Palestine, it was Russian, together with German, that I chose.

Having, more or less, learned the language, boasting a Degree in it and steeped in the tangled beauties of Dostoyevsky and Tolstoy, with typical bureaucratic indifference, I was immediately sent to Malaya for three years during the troubles there. An experience, indeed, but very far removed from the Russian Steppes. On my return, however, after considerable effort, I did manage to get attached to the Russian Army in Eastern Germany where both languages were useful in extricating myself from some mildly hilarious situations. Stints learning, and then teaching, at the Army Staff College followed before leaving Her Majesty's Service, finding, dare I say it, life a little dull on the North German plains.

I then entered political life – a great change. I joined the Conservative Research Department, in due course finding myself Head of Overseas Affairs there and then Political Secretary to Sir

Alec Douglas-Home at the Foreign Office, accompanying him on his many foreign visits, including Russia.

It was at this stage that my three main interests in life – Russia, military affairs and politics – began to coalesce. I remembered some extraordinary situations in which I found myself as a young, very young, officer in Palestine. In retrospect, I had very little idea why I was there. What was the process by which solemn decisions in carpeted rooms taken by mysterious figures in secret culminated in blood or, often, farce? Having worked closely for Heath, Douglas-Home and other luminaries, I had some idea of the often tortured channels through which decisions eventually emerged. But why the killing? Good intentions so often seem to result in chaos, luckily not so much when I was there, but in the past? and in the future? Why the hatred? Did leaders and nations never learn from evident past mistakes? And why do alliances, ostensibly with common causes, so often fall apart?

So many of these interests seemed to come together in the Allied Intervention in Russia in 1918/19 about which my father's swordstick had originally whetted my curiosity. I began to read what I could about the episode. The more I read the more it seemed to me to have involved issues of stunning relevance to the world we live in and to lay bare the stark contrasts between the often agonized decisions taken by people far from the scene and those, often ignorant, pawns on both sides of the action.

Some twenty years ago I interviewed a number of people who were there, mostly as soldiers, but some in other capacities. I then discovered that there was a mass of material in the Imperial War Museum, including some sixty diaries written by those who had participated, as soldiers, sailors and airmen. There were also a number of learned tomes on these and related matters, together with some personal published accounts of the fighting. And I had my father's journal. There was no lack of material.

Some eighty-four years after the event, many people do not realize that, shortly after the Revolution, Soviet Russia was invaded by armies, varying greatly in size, from some sixteen countries, including Britain, the United States, France and Japan. Some people have a vague notion that something of the sort occurred but have no idea either of the scale of the attacks or of their geographical spread. In fact, attacks came in from the north, east, south and west. Motives were very varied: failure was universal. Many British servicemen found themselves in the most extraordinary situations without any clear idea of why they were there at all. I decided to start the book with a few snapshots of some of these situations scattered around the landmass of the old Imperial Russia. Then there would be a chapter outlining the political background, followed by a series of chapters examining the various incursions in some detail. Finally, there would be a conclusion which would include a reference to possible lessons to be learnt from this extraordinary, and little known, episode.

Chapter One

SIX STORIES

The North (Archangel)

In early 1919 Charles Hudson[1]* found himself acting as Brigade Major to Brigadier General Turner who commanded a mixed force holding a railway line some ninety miles south of Archangel in North Russia against attacks by the Red Army. The main element of Turner's force consisted of four White Russian battalions, two in the front line and two in reserve, together with a Polish machine-gun company. Before General Turner's arrival the force had been commanded by a French Officer, Commandant Lucas.

The Headquarters was in the large village of Obozerskaya, with an outpost further south at the village of Bolshie Ozerki. In March the French Commandant had heard of the approach towards Bolshie Ozerki of a Bolshevik column. According to his British staff, he sat down to write 'An Appreciation of the Situation', aided by liberal potions of brandy. As his morale alternatively rose and fell as a result of the rumours of the strength of the enemy and the effects of the brandy he destroyed and rewrote his conclusions. In-between times he could be heard striding up and down his office compartment muttering, "What would Foch do?" By nightfall he had decided not only that Foch would withdraw from the village, but that he would withdraw his Headquarters train from Obozerskaya to a siding ten miles

* See Notes on p.196.

5

north. Orders were given that the train was to be prepared to move at short notice. The British staff were mortified by this order and the Brigade Major, Staff Captain and Signals Officer crept down to the engine at night and, while one held the attention of the engine driver, the others poured boiling water on the rails further down the line. This, they had been told, would have the effect of spinning the icebound wheels of the engine when it reached the doctored track. In fact the Bolshevik column, if it existed, never turned up and next day General Ironside, the British Commander in Chief in North Russia, replaced Commandant Lucas with Brigadier General Turner.

On the evening of 20 July Hudson was working in his office just before dinner when his Chief Clerk, a Russian, crept in furtively, keeping below the level of the windows. The blinds having been drawn at the Chief Clerk's request, he said that a note had been handed to him by a Russian private soldier, obviously having mistaken him for a Russian Sergeant Major in one of the reserve battalions to whom it had been addressed. The note made it clear that the enemy would attack on the railway at dawn on 23 July. The two White Russian battalions in the line would offer no resistance and would arrest their officers just before the attack, shooting any who resisted. The writer, who signed with a codename, said that he anticipated no difficulty in overrunning the remainder of the brigade who would be taken entirely by surprise, and for this reason only the forward battalions had been informed of the plan. The note also said that a special column which was to attack Force Headquarters was already in position in the forest and that the recipient of the note had to arrange to cut a gap in the wire, at the place arranged, during the night preceding the attack. In a final paragraph the writer said that arrangements had been made for communications to be cut in good time.

The only absolutely reliable troops were about twenty British at Headquarters, the Polish company of machine gunners and, possibly the crew of an armoured train who were Russian sailors and, as such, on bad terms with the Russian soldiers.

It was clearly vital to relieve the two forward battalions as soon as possible. Having finished the dinner as normal, in order not to excite the suspicion of the Russians who were serving them, a plan was hatched whereby the two reserve battalions would be paraded and told that cholera had broken out in the two forward battalions and that relief would be carried out by train, company by company, immediately after the parade. As each forward company approached the station, which would be surrounded by the Polish machine gunners, the men would be told that the armoured train had broken down, blocking the line, and they were to get out of the train, leaving their equipment behind them. They would then be marched, disarmed, to prisoner-of-war cages under Polish escort. If any attempt to resist was made, the armoured train and the Poles would be used to overpower them. The senior White Russian Colonel would be in charge.

The whole affair went exactly according to plan. Eight times the manoeuvre was put into operation and every time it worked smoothly. However, it remained important to find the names of the leaders of the conspiracy. As each company was disarmed, the Russian Colonel asked for the names of these men. When no one volunteered any information he told them he would pick on any man in the ranks, count ten men down from him and that man would be shot. When the first batch of men were singled out, a Polish party marched them away into the forest. This was followed by a burst of fire. Hudson, who was observing, although he knew that the men were not in fact being shot, was staggered by the phlegmatic way in which the majority of the men, even those who knew they were about to be shot, faced their apparent fate. At intervals, for hour after hour, this process went on. It was getting on for ten o'clock that night when the last company was marched away and still no information was forthcoming. Hudson wrote in his journal, 'As the last company passed us, a young boy, a bugler, broke away, approached the Colonel and myself and, having been promised a release from the army and a return to his village, told us who the ringleaders were.'

When the Bolsheviks attacked on the morning of the 23rd, they were faced by the reserve battalions which had been moved to the Front, and which repulsed the attack. As for the potential mutineers, after heavy interrogation, including, it was admitted by the Russian Colonel, some torture, a large number of NCOs and men were executed.

Hudson was extremely unhappy about the proceedings, but the British had always made it clear that they were in no way responsible for the discipline of the Russians who had their own code of law. The method of execution, too, must have been revolting, although he did not know it at the time. The firing party consisted of two Lewis machine guns fired at ground level. They could not aim higher than at their victims' legs.

When Hudson expostulated about Russian methods, the Russian Colonel replied bitterly, 'You British don't realize what we are up against. You come out here from comfortably secure homes, knowing full well you can return to them. For us, it's a good deal more that just our own individual life and death. The issue affects the whole of Russia.' And he went on to explain the methods used by the Bolsheviks in their bid to take over Russia and, he said, the world. Hudson was silenced.

Orders were received in early August for the total evacuation from North Russia of all British, and other Allied, servicemen. The theory was that the anti-Bolshevik Russians would take over from the Allied troops, that they would defeat the Reds and set up a Government. However, virtually nobody in touch with the reality of the situation believed this.

On about 10 September Hudson's Brigade Headquarters embarked on a train at Obozerskaya en route to Archangel where they were destined to embark on a ship to return to Britain. The Commanding Officer of the White Russian battalion which had nearly mutinied and with whom Hudson had become very friendly in spite of his dismissive attitudes towards the normal tenets of military law, Russian or British, stood in full uniform on the platform at the salute. As the train drew out, he shot himself.

The North (Murmansk)

Charles Painter,[2] born in 1900, joined the Army as a boy in November 1916. He was trained as a Lewis Gunner and joined the Middlesex Regiment. In early 1919, still a private soldier, he was told his battalion was going to Russia – no one explained why. He arrived in Murmansk on 9 April 1919. On arrival, they were told that they were there to help the White Russians because Britain had £1,000,000 worth of stores in a warehouse in Murmansk and 'we had to get it back'. He was serving in a company of about 500 men under a Major Drew. They had another officer who 'was not much good as he had been a prisoner of war for nearly the whole war and knew nothing about modern warfare'. However, they had a very good sergeant.

After two months or so they started by train down the line towards Petrograd. Painter was one of the guards to a General, of whose name he was not sure, on a separate coach. They got as far as Medvyezha Gora where they were told that there was some trouble at a village called Lambuski which was to the east. So they were detached to deal with the trouble. However nothing seemed to happen when they got there. They had a marvellous time. They were there for two months doing nothing very much except fishing with grenades.

When they had been in Murmansk they had not seen much of the Russians except that they were able to make a lot of money by selling almost everything they could lay their hands on to them. They got about five shillings for a pair of old socks and Army rum was sold for five or six or seven pounds a bottle. They had a ration but they generally managed to get their hands on a bit more. The whole time he was in Russia Painter only drew forty pounds pay and made all the rest of his money by selling things to the Russians. They even sold tea leaves. When they had been used they dried them and wrapped them up and then sold them.

After their time in Lambuski they went on to Soroko. They were now marching, carrying all their kit. There was a Salvation Army canteen on the train which was marvellous and from which they bought cigarettes and so on.

When they were at Soroko they got held up and shelled. It was not very effective fire but one shell landed on a fire where he was cooking a tin of kippers. Luckily it did not explode, but his kippers were ruined.

The furthest they got was about 40 versts (twenty-seven miles) from Petrograd. When they got there, for no apparent reason, they were told to withdraw to Murmansk so they went back, fighting a rearguard action the whole way. They had the Americans with them throughout. The American battalion consisted of a civilian company which constructed railway lines. The manager was the Colonel and the foremen were sergeant majors and officers. There was no formality, they just called each other 'buddy' all the time. As they withdrew, the British burnt the bridges behind them which the Americans had just constructed. 'It all seemed a bit silly.'

They were in Murmansk for a month or so. 'We left alone most of the British stores which were there but we helped ourselves to most of the rest. We had at least four kit bags each stuffed full of tinned food, clothes and a whole mass of equipment of all kinds. We then got a cattle boat home.'

At no time did Painter really know why he was in Russia or what he was doing there. He merely did what he was told. His main aim seemed to be to lay his hands on as much loot as he possibly could.

The East

Colonel Riviere[3] had been in the Loyal Regiment in Mesopotamia in 1918. A paper came round asking for volunteers for the British Force at Vladivostok in Eastern Russia, the objective of which was to get supplies of military equipment to the White Russians. He and one or two others had volunteered. About Christmas of 1918 he received a telegram ordering him to Vladivostok 'forthwith'. He was going to take part in a horse race for the Brigade Cup in about three days time so he asked his CO whether forthwith meant that he could wait for three days. The CO said yes and he won the race. He then went down a river, the name of which he could not remember, to Baghdad. He then got another boat down the Tigris to Basra where he got a boat on to Bombay. Another boat to Hong Kong, another boat to Shanghai and then finally another boat belonging to the Canadian Pacific Railway from Shanghai to Vladivostok stopping on the way at Japan, although the Japanese were very suspicious and would not let them off the boat.

When he arrived in Vladivostok he found there were a whole mass of different nationalities there, including the Italians, the French, the Japanese and the Americans. The objective was to unload the supplies which came off boats arriving at Vladivostok and send them up the railway to Omsk where they were to be received by the White Russians. The British were commanded by Sir Alfred Knox and the Russians by Admiral Kolchak. Riviere was a Staff Captain working under a Brigadier Blair. He thought that the British managed to get most of their stuff up to Omsk whereas the Americans and the others did not seem to bother much. The Czechs had changed sides and were on their way to Vladivostok. The supplies were mainly guns, rifles and ammunition but he remembered one consignment of Canadian horses. They did not know what to do with the horses since they had no one to look after them. They found some Cossacks wandering around and used them for a bit but they were 'no good at all'. They then got hold of some German prisoners of war and used them. 'They were very good.'

Riviere was out there for no less than fifteen months but never really managed to get far beyond Vladivostok. Eventually the White Russians collapsed. The Czechs came back through Vladivostok and went off 'somewhere' before the Reds arrived. They seemed to behave fairly well but took half of the headquarters building which was occupied by General Blair's Headquarters and was the best building in the town. They asked if they could have a typewriter with Russian letters. Riviere gave them one but the question of payment came up. He asked for Chinese dollars but the Russians hadn't got any and offered him Omsk roubles. They were no good so he gave the typewriter to the Reds who were very pleased. It does not seem to have occurred to him that the Reds might have cut his throat since he had been giving supplies to their enemies. Eventually, however, things got rather bad and a number of British soldiers were killed. He saw their bodies on the railway station steps. So he and a Captain Savory thought they'd better leave. They found a train but there was no engine. Eventually they found an engine

11

but then there was no driver. So they got hold of a Russian driver and, at the point of a revolver, told him to drive. Then about thirty of them set off in this train, went to the Russian border with China near Harbin and then went on, apparently with a Chinese driver at this stage, down through Mukden and Tientsin to Peking. For the first part of the journey through Manchuria the Japanese had been in charge and had been very difficult but the Chinese were 'much nicer'.

When Riviere was at Vladivostok one of the things he had to do was give out medals to the Allies. He and his Brigadier had worked out a list which included a Japanese General. He was to get a KCB. However, shortly after he was presented with this medal he came in looking rather embarrassed and said that he had read the British Army list and he had seen that most of the Generals got GCBs. So they sent a wire to 'the war house' and received the reply, 'Give him his G'. However, when it came to give out a number of medals, it turned out that many of those who were to receive them had changed sides so a large number of medals were not actually presented. Riviere took these medals with him all the way back to England. The normal train from Vladivostok to Omsk took about six weeks. However, a very flamboyant character called Colonel Rodzianko, a great horseman, was put in charge of one of the trains and he got it through in six days. Apparently he told each station master as he went along that if he didn't move on quickly he would 'thrash him'.

Colonel Riviere did not seem to know anything much about what was happening in Eastern Russia or what they were all doing there. He said that some of the Russians were, 'good fellows', some of them were 'bad chaps'.

When he got to Peking the Chinese Navy gave a party for them. He was very struck by the beauty of the Chinese ladies! Eventually they went down by train from Peking to Shanghai and went back to England where he was immediately sent out to Ireland to deal with the Sinn Féin.

When told that he seemed to have had a very interesting life, he said that he didn't think so, 'Everything was quite normal for those days.'

The South East

In January 1918 Lieutenant Blacker[4], later to become famous as the first man to fly over Everest, found himself in Tashkent, the capital of Russian Turkestan, as part of a mission headed by Sir George McCartney, consisting of a few diplomats and sixteen soldiers, all but two belonging to the Queen Victoria's Own Corps of Guides from the Indian Army. It had been rumoured that there were tens of thousands of tons of cotton ready baled in the warehouses of Turkestan and the aim of McCartney's mission was somehow to prevent this priceless raw material, which could be used for the production of gun cotton, from reaching Germany, either through Moscow or the Caucasus. The situation in the area was one of total confusion. There were thousands of discharged Hungarian, German and Austrian prisoners of war rampaging around the area, many of them by that time supporters of the Bolsheviks. There were large numbers of Cossacks fighting the Reds for their independence. There were Afghans and Tartars taking for themselves what they could get in the chaos. There was the Red Army, and the Turks were approaching the area from the west. The situation was livened up every now and again as the Soviets, determined to remind the citizens of Tashkent who was ruling the city, would hurtle through the streets in an armoured car, its powerful exhaust shrieking and its machine gun firing off in the air, while those present hid hastily round a corner.

Blacker and a colleague were sitting a café listening to an orchestra comprised of released Austrian prisoners of war who were playing the Marseillaise with much gusto – at that time the Bolsheviks were trying to ape the French Revolution in word and deed. One of the orchestra, seeing that Blacker and his friend looked somewhat bemused, came up to them and asked what nationality they were. On being told that they were British, he said that they would immediately play the British National Anthem. He went back to his orchestra and, shortly afterwards, the whole ensemble, with great authority and passion, struck up with 'It's a long way to Tipperary'. Everyone in the café rose to their feet in honour of the British people.

Blacker was seeing the Soviets twice a week in an apparent dialogue of the deaf, as neither side either understood or trusted the other. On one occasion the local Soviet President asked him what the British House of Commons thought of the Soviet Federation of Turkestan Republics. Virtually certain that very few Members of the British House of Commons would have heard of Turkestan at all and those that had would probably think it was in Tibet, Blacker assured the President that the British Parliament extended its warmest sympathy and heartfelt good wishes to those newer democracies struggling like them against despotism, capitalism, imperialism, monarchism and any other 'isms' the President had in mind.

The South

Bob Vincent[5] was born in a country village, Chilbolton, in Hampshire. Aged eighteen he was called up in September 1918 and served with the Royal Warwickshire Regiment. He volunteered to join the British Military Mission in South Russia. He only did so because his best friend had asked him to volunteer, saying, 'Life in the Army in peacetime is rather dull.' Travelling via Boulogne, Marseilles, Port Said, Constantinople and Baku, the Mission finished up at Novorossisk on the Black Sea where they were guarding clothing and medical stores which, they were told, were for the White Army. They saw some British Tank Corps people with Whippet tanks and 'one big diamond shape tank'. There were also some RAF there, together with some men from the Naval Brigade who, for some totally inexplicable reason, ran the trains. They were sent to Rostov and some of them went on to Kharkov to act as servants to 'some of our officers who were advisers to the White Army'. However, the Red Army kept on advancing and they retreated to Taganrog, where they spent Christmas 1919, back to Rostov and then on to Ekaterinodar, where the head of the British Military Mission, General Holman, had his headquarters. The Russians were under martial law and Vincent kept on seeing Russians 'hanging in various courtyards'. He was not sure what they had done, but he knew that if a Russian was caught stealing from the British stores he would be instantly executed, so the British did not report them. 'A lot of Russians were wearing British military uniform and it was difficult to know whether or not to salute someone dressed as a British officer.' Their own officer told them that 'the next time you see a sack of potatoes coming through the gate, you salute it'. There was a lot of typhus about 'and some of our lads died of it'.

He was then detailed with two other soldiers and a medical orderly to go backwards and forwards from Ekaterinodar to Novorossisk in one coach of a train which was painted with the words 'British Military Mission', collecting odd British people who were stuck at Ekaterinodar and people who were ill and the odd businessman who seemed to be floating around. Each journey took him about two or three days and they went backwards and forwards numerous times. By this time it was the spring of 1920. There was no coal so the train had to stop every now and again and pick up wood which was lying in stacks beside the railway. They had two stoves and would cook the food on the journey in the coach. The food mostly consisted of bully beef. Their main job was to stop others trying to get on their coach. There were 'hundreds and hundreds' of Russians trying to get on any train to get out. Russians were on the roof and on the buffers. The had about thirty per coach.

Things gradually got worse and the Reds got closer and closer. The British then left Novorossisk in a ship called the *Field Marshal*. Or the main body did. They had to form a cordon on the quay to keep off the ship the thousands of Russians who were trying to escape. When nearly all were embarked there were twenty left behind for the final guard. Vincent was one of the twenty. He was a bit worried. However, they went out along the sea wall where they found a British torpedo boat and they boarded her. They went to Feodosiya where they met up with the *Field Marshal*. They stayed a week or so there. They were inspected by the General Holman. However, he did not speak to them or tell them what they were doing, why they were there or whether they had done well or done badly. They then boarded the *Centaur* and went to Sebastopol. Here they did more guard duty and a number of parades which impressed the Russians very

15

much. The Russians were particularly impressed by the few Scots they had with them who were in kilts. They also guarded the hospital. 'We had quite a good time in Sebastopol – we did a number of parades – mainly funerals. We also went to Balaclava. Captain Barnard asked us if we would like to go up the 'Valley of Death', which we did. We also saw the museum at Sebastopol which the Russians had. It showed the battle of Sebastopol in panoramic form. You stood on the top and looked down on the panoramic painting inside with pictures of the British and Russian troops. You then looked over the rampart and saw exactly the same picture now. The harbour was full of British ships.' Then they went on to Lemnos where long-serving soldiers were dropped off to help with a White Russian refugee camp that was there. They then went back to Port Said and left in an Italian ship for Southampton.

When they were in Russia, the British soldiers had a rum ration nearly every day. They were paid in roubles – the equivalent of £1 a week. When they arrived they got 200 roubles and when they left it was 2,500, but they could not buy anything with this money. When they eventually left they were told they could change £5 worth but they kept the rest and gave it to their friends when they got home. At one stage Vincent had to escort two soldiers who were going back to Constantinople to be court martialled. They crossed the Black Sea on a local boat which was very full. When they got to Constantinople they handed the soldiers over – incidentally, he had no idea what their crime was and didn't think it worth asking them – and they hung around Constant, as he called it, for a bit. 'There was a tram which went in an S up the hill but there were steps which you could walk up instead of going by tram.' On each side of the steps were stalls and he and his pal took it in turns to get the stallholder on one side in hot conversation while the other nicked a few things from the other stall. At the top of the steps there was a YMCA! There were lots of British troops in Constant. They lived on bully beef and biscuits most of the time when they were in Russia. They made it into a large stew and thought it was very good. 'I never really met any Russians at all, or had any idea why I was there.

However, I enjoyed it. It was the most exciting period of my life and a marvelous opportunity to travel!'

The South-West

It was August 1918 and Captain Missen's[6] twenty-first birthday. With the bulk of his battalion of the 7th North Staffordshire Regiment, of which he was Adjutant, he was on board the *President Kruger*, a 1,000 ton boat belonging to the White Russians, on his way north on the Caspian Sea from Enzeli in Persia to the oil port of Baku in Russian Azerbaijan. They were part of Dunster Force, commanded by General Dunsterville, and their immediate mission was to go to the relief of the Central Caspian Revolutionary Government – a body of Armenians and Azerbaijanis who had shortly before taken power back from the Bolsheviks in a coup. They were besieged by the Turkish Caucasus – Islam Army. (There was also a division of German troops somewhere around and many German/Austrian prisoners of war who had been released and who were not sure what to do next.)

A twenty-first birthday was something to celebrate, wherever he might be, and Missen looked round to find someone to celebrate it with him. To his surprise he found that there were two others on the boat whose twenty-first birthday it also was. One was a French-speaking Russian Air Force officer whose loyalties were to the old regime in Russia and the other was a charming Armenian, apparently a businessman, clearly very able but also very communist. His name was Mikoyan. An Englishman, a Tsarist Russian and a communist Russian. They had a great party there on the deck as the sun set over the Caspian. They drank champagne. Missen remembered it well. They talked a lot of politics and wondered which philosophy was gong to win and what would happen to them in the future. In fact, Missen finished up as a County Chief Education Officer, the Russian Tsarist officer was never seen again – he may well have died fighting for his outworn creed – and Mikoyan became Chairman of the Presidium. Which philosophy won? Certainly not the Tsarist (or its equivalent) and, now, certainly not the

17

communist, although it has taken some eighty years to prove that. As for Missen's philosophy, he did not really have one: he was very English.

His battalion fought hard to save Baku from the Turks, but eventually had to be evacuated back to Enzeli.

But that was not the end of the story. After the Armistice of November 1918 Missen's battalion was sent back to Baku in order to drive out the Turks who were now masquerading as soldiers of the Azerbaijani Republic. The Turks eventually left in February 1919. But Missen and his battalion remained in Baku waiting for decisions from Versailles as to what would happen next. It was a very pleasant time. The Opera House was re-opened and he saw a new production every fortnight. Money was a problem. There were Azerbaijani roubles, Kerensky roubles, Tsarist roubles and Communist roubles. Because of the delicate political situation the British soldiers were not allowed to carry arms, an odd situation in an area where nobody knew who was friend or foe or what was going to happen next. There were also still some 40,000 German and Austrian ex-prisoners or war floating around looking for food and money.

Possibly the most bizarre problem which Missen faced was getting suitable food for his soldiers. Black bread and fresh fish were available but not popular, but the main complaint was the quantities of caviare with which they were supplied. The soldiers would not eat it.

Chapter Two

THE POLITICAL BACKGROUND

Why were these British servicemen placed in these extraordinary situations? In terms of world politics it could well be argued that the Allied intervention in Russia was a sideshow when compared to the tumultuous slaughter of the First World War. But it was not a sideshow to those who took part, nor was it so to the relatives of those who were killed. Nor, it will be argued in this book, was it peripheral to the developing saga of Bolshevik (later called Communist) rule over the great land mass to be known as the Soviet Union which was to play such a powerful, if not dominating, role in the evolution of world politics in the second half of the twentieth century.

It is difficult to imagine a more confused situation than that in Europe in the aftermath of the second Russian Revolution in November 1917. The vast tidal wave of the Great War was overtaken, arguably, by an even greater event in terms of its ultimate significance – the Russian Revolution. Regimes, previously seemingly impregnable, were spewed lifeless on the shore like so much flotsam. Currents of change swept unpredictably across the world leaving chaos, death and destruction behind them in whole areas of our troubled planet. Eventually the immediate convulsions calmed down, but the danger of further upheavals remained to erupt again in 1939.

It is not surprising that the institutions of the old Europe, whether those of the Central Powers or of the Allies and the United States, were totally unable to cope with the situation as it developed over the years. There was dissension, muddle, indecision and a total lack of understanding of what was happening. Almost everybody wanted to get in on the act and to grab what they could for themselves. Good intentions there were in some quarters, notably by the Americans, but they did indeed pave the road to Hell: the eventual result in the late 1930s with Hitler and Stalin supreme was indeed hell on earth for millions of human beings.

One thing is certain: the Allied intervention in Russia failed to achieve any of the very many objectives it was variously given (except arguably the denial of Baku oil to the Germans in 1918). The Baltic States would almost certainly have achieved their independence anyway. Mistakes there clearly were, massive, continuous and all-pervading. Indeed, it is difficult to find any action taken by any of the Allies (apart from the various with-drawals) which is to be applauded. Of course it is always easy to be critical from the security and knowledge of the retro-spective observer. No doubt, to those who made the decisions, there were always good, even apparently imperative, reasons for what they decided. Furthermore, the pressures on the Allied leaders, particularly in early 1918 when the Allies came close to losing the war, were enormous. But nevertheless there must surely be some rules which should be followed in international affairs, even if only that it is best to find out what is happening on the ground before taking irrevocable action. It must surely also be wrong to give contradictory orders – and so on. As the story unfolds, the reader may well find it almost incredible that seasoned and experienced statesmen, politicians and soldiers alike should make so many elementary but colossal errors. It must, however, be remembered throughout that nothing in the experience of these people had prepared them for what confronted them. They were treading completely new ground. Perhaps we can learn something from their experiences and those of the men who had to carry out their orders. In the following chapters we shall see much of what actually happened on the ground and how totally different, often, things appear to those doing the fighting to the situation as imagined by those who give orders from the security of the office or conference table.

One of the greatest problems that had to be faced by the Allies in trying to cope with the Russian Revolution lay in the apparent impossibility of achieving any kind of unity of purpose. Those involved, apart from the various, often bitterly antagonistic, Russian anti-Bolshevik factions, included the British, French, Americans, Japanese, Canadians, Australians, Serbs, Poles, Finns, the Baltic States, Greeks, Rumanians, Italians, Czechs and even the Chinese. There were very different views about what should or should not be done not only between virtually all these countries but also, often within the political structures of the nations concerned. This was particularly true of Britain where those two towering figures Lloyd George and Churchill were in almost total disagreement about everything to do with the Russian problem. There were of course disagreements within the Bolshevik leadership too, but Lenin and Trotsky between them dominated the Red scene and the eventual de facto split of responsibility between them – Lenin dealt with political and Trotsky with military matters – worked well.

The real difficulty in the Allied camp lay in the very different experiences which the countries concerned had had and the impact of geography. Britain with its channel and world empire; France with its memories of 1870, its common border with Germany and the colossal casualties it had suffered in the 1914-18 war; America, brash and young, just having joined the war under its idealistic President; Japan, far from the scene, testing its muscles after its defeat of Russia in 1904 and looking for a place in the sun: how could any agreed policy be achieved with motivations so varied? Within a country it may just be possible to achieve a cabinet policy so that ministers take responsibility for decisions with which they themselves do not agree. But it is immeasurably more difficult with international alliances however apparently successful they may be. The perceived supreme national interest will always predominate in the last instance as long as the nation state exists. And if a spurious unity is forced on to people who do not accept it, it will not endure – as proved to be the case with both the Ottoman and Austro-Hungarian Empires and, indeed, to an extent, with the British Empire.

In any event, as will become apparent as the book proceeds,

the Allies were in fact unable to agree on policy at almost every stage. There were occasions when the cracks were papered over – but the results then were even worse. When those involved in a joint venture are given conflicting orders to those of their colleagues from other nations (as happened in virtually every situation when the Americans were involved) the confusion, bitterness and lack of joint purpose can be disastrous.

One of the problems is that politicians and diplomats by their very nature are inured to compromise and the search for a way round difficulties. In international affairs they serve their countries badly if they obscure divisions which surface later in far more difficult circumstances.

A further, and apparently endemic disease, which seemed to afflict virtually all national leaders at that time was that of wishful thinking. Wherever one looks one sees false optimism. Even Lenin, that great realist, really believed that world revolution would follow the Bolshevik successes in Russia and many of his mistakes stem from that wholly mistaken dogma.

It is of course impossible to be a leader without eternal optimism. Belief in the probability of success is essential if one is to convince others and the dividing line between wishful thinking and a generally optimistic view of the future is a fine one. But there can rarely have been so many leaders who were so wrong in their predictions of the future and who have based policy on such a misunderstanding of the true situation which confronted them. Only the Bolsheviks approached anywhere near achieving their aims and, as has already been said, their success was limited to Russia, was accompanied by starvation, misery and general privations far worse than they had expected and, as it has turned out, was to end in ignominious failure, albeit some seventy years later.

None of those participants in these great events whose stories were told in Chapter One were killed in the fighting. They survived to tell their tales. But millions did not. There was death, starvation and misery on a massive scale – all to very little purpose. Very few of any of the Allied soldiers who fought in Russia or who went there for reasons other than fighting during this period understood what they were doing or why they were doing it. Their motives were very varied. Most went there because they were told to, some went for adventure, some for material gain of one sort or another. In retrospect it seems as if many of them were pawns in a game, apparently played by blindfolded players on a shifting board under changing rules. Decisions then, and often now, were taken by those who had fought their way up to the top of the greasy political pole, the repercussions of which were totally different to what was envisaged and individuals, then as now and always, were swept away, sometimes vainly protesting as their heads bobbed above the flood. Far too often, then as now, political decisions were taken with the individuals who were involved on the ground being thought of only in stereotyped cliché terms – the Reds, the Whites, the French and so on. The submerging of the individual into an apparently totally supine prototype leads, and has led throughout the centuries, to much cruelty and unhappiness.

Of course, the great decision as far as the Allies were concerned was whether or not to intervene in the Russian maelstrom at all. And, having done so, whether or not to withdraw and, if so, when. The fact is that intervention in a civil war is nearly always, as so many countries have discovered over the years, mistaken; it certainly was in Russia in 1918. It may well, as it did in Russia, lead to precisely the opposite of what its sponsors intended and it is always far more difficult to get out than to get in. One could almost say 'Intervene in haste, repent at leisure.'

The Russian Revolutions of 1917 were major and definitive events which decisively changed the course of world history. However, the conventional view of a Russia, uniformly sullen and oppressed, struggling free from a despotic uncaring aristocracy is untrue as, of course, are many conventional views. The truth, in so far as there exists such a thing as objective truth, is very much more complex.

The Russian state had grown inexorably over the centuries, a process which began at the end of the thirteenth century when 'Muscovy', as it came to be called, consisted of an area about the size of Wales, including Moscow. The expansion was comparatively rapid in the early stages and the bulk of northern Asia, including just about the whole of Siberia, was part of Imperial Russia by the end of the seventeenth century. The large area east of the Caspian Sea together with the hinterland north and west of Vladivostok was not settled until the nineteenth century. This was happening, interestingly enough, at the same time as the Americans were colonizing their continent, and there are many parallels between the American and Russian periods of colonization. Having completed their colonial empire, the Russians then embarked on their own industrial revolution. From an almost entirely rural economy Russia turned herself very quickly into one of the leading industrial countries of the world. In the last decade of the nineteenth century there was a colossal increase of industrial activity. Vast deposits of coal and iron were found and private capital flowed into Russia from the West. This led, later, to the great concern of the Allies, and particularly of the French whose bourgeoisie had heavily invested there, when Lenin repudiated all Russian debts after the Revolution. But perhaps the greatest effect of the industrial revolution in Russia, which was to become a decisive factor in the revolutionary situation which developed later, was the creation of a large urban population. There was suddenly a great and apparently insatiable demand for workers in the towns. The fact that virtually none of them were trained for factory work added to the influx as two or three untrained workers produced what one trained man could have managed. The urban population between 1863 and 1914 rose from 6,000,000 to 18,600,000 and their grievances were a fertile ground for revolutionary activity and for the ideas of Karl Marx. The creation of a large urban proletariat was to be a major cause of the victory of the Reds over the Whites in the Civil War. The Reds were predominantly urban whereas many of the Whites were peasants who, in the summer of 1919, left their ranks to return home in order to gather in the harvest[1].

The system of government which had grown up over the years with an autocratic Tsar presiding over a country which, it has been said, resembled nothing so much as a large military academy with its civil servants all wearing uniform in a highly structured hierarchy of rank, was quite unable to cope with the changed circumstances, not only of industrialization but of the increasingly vocal intelligentsia and the influx of liberal ideas from the West. The move to Western capitalism brought with it its opponent – socialism. The Tsarist Secret Police were of course active in suppressing any signs of revolutionary activity, but at a congress held in London in July 1903 a decisive step was taken when the extremists, under Lenin, prevailed over the moderates under the leadership of Plekhanov. Hence the names – Bolsheviks (the men of the majority) and Mensheviks (the men of the minority). Lenin's view was that the Revolution should be led by an elite of theorists and activists at the centre rather than by a mass movement arising from the grass roots.

In spite of the autocratic nature of the regime there was a general upsurge of liberal activities and ideas and political parties of one sort or another. It would be tedious here to follow in detail the kaleidoscopic gyrations of the various official and unofficial organizations which operated openly and secretly under the Tsarist autocracy at the turn of the century.

At no point, however, was Tsarist repression of anything like the same order as existed under Stalin towards the end of his period of power. Under the Tsars, there were of course executions and dissidents were exiled. But there was none of the mass slaughter and the sheer terror under which a whole nation was cowed into total subjection. Under the Tsars, people did write and distribute what were regarded as subversive documents. There were strikes and many other manifestations of profound discontent. Under Stalin there was silence and even later under Brezhnev the few dissenting voices were nothing compared to the scale of the liberal opposition in Tsarist Russia.

After the debacle of the highly unpopular, and lost, Russo/Japanese war of 1904 which had been brought about by the wish of Tsar Nicholas and some of his Ministers to dominate East Asia, there had been a concerted move by the liberals who were becoming more and more powerful to bring about a far greater degree of liberty and democratic control. The liberals were joined by a whole range of other interests including the professional classes and factory workers. A peaceful march on the Winter Palace was fired upon on 22 January 1905 and many people were killed. This was followed by wholesale unrest throughout the country. There were numerous strikes, thirteen railway lines stopped functioning and the Tsar's uncle, the Governor General of Moscow, was murdered. The Tsar was forced to concede the calling together of a National Assembly or Duma.

It began to sit on 1 May 1906. It found itself in almost total opposition to the Government at every point and it was dissolved on 21 July. There was a further relapse into reactionary autocracy and 600 revolutionaries were executed. The second Duma, which met in March 1907, showed a great shift to the political left – the comparatively right wing Cadets only had 123 seats whereas Labour had 200 and the two revolutionary parties – the Socialist Revolutionaries and the Social Democrats – had 89 seats between them. The second Duma in its turn was dissolved and the franchise was again restricted by decree. The third Duma, which also met in 1907, consisted largely of Conservative representatives of one sort or another. But it too began to attack the Government for its inefficiency and the arbitrary nature of its rule. It gained much influence in the country and it and the fourth Duma, elected in 1912, was able to bring about a transformation in the economic and social life of the country. Government revenues increased fast, education was made accessible to all and great strides were made in land reform.

As far as the Russians were concerned the First World War broke out because of their fears that the Germans were out to subjugate the Slavs in Eastern Europe – fears which were well justified. The Russian intelligentsia had never had much, if any, interest in Eastern Asia, but historically they had very close association with and interest in Pan-Slavism in the West. When the war broke out after the assassination of the Archduke Francis Ferdinand at Sarajevo on 28 June 1914, following the Austrian attack on Serbia and Russian partial mobilization, it was extremely popular throughout Russia. The Tsar's popularity soared and Russia rejoiced.

The war was, however, a disaster for Russia. She did have a few successes initially but her Army was completely unequipped for war on the scale which confronted it. Ammunition and equipment, transport, leadership, staff work – all were vastly inadequate. In the first ten months of the war the Russians lost no less than 3,800,000 men.

A meeting of the Duma in November 1916 was dominated by denunciations of the Government by delegates of all political hues. Revolution was clearly approaching but the Tsar appeared to be oblivious to the dangers surrounding him. In early March 1917 large-scale disorders broke out and on 15 March, having tried in vain to retrieve the situation by force, the Tsar abdicated in favour of his brother, the Grand Duke Nicholas who, however, refused to accept the throne. A provisional Government, formed by members of the Duma, took power with support from the Soviets (councils of workers and soldiers) and throughout the eight-month period of the Provisional Government there was a dual system of government, so that the two bodies jostled each other for power.

The fall of the Tsar and the arrival of a new, if provisional, Government, still dedicated to the cause of winning the war, was received with euphoria, not only within Russia, but throughout the world. It was hoped by the Allies that the Russian war effort would receive a much needed boost and there was little sympathy for the Tsar, who was seen almost everywhere as the leader of a tyrannical regime whose demise was long overdue. The USA, Britain and France very quickly recognized the new Government. Lloyd George welcomed the new Russia as one of those countries 'which based their institutions upon representative Government'. The USA was on the point of entering the war and President Wilson welcomed 'the heartening things that have been happening within the last few weeks in Russia'. He praised 'the great, generous Russian people who have been added in all their native majesty and might to the forces that are fighting for freedom in the world, for justice and for peace. Here is a fit partner for a League of Honour.' Virtually the only reservations were felt by King George V who was upset by the overthrow of his cousin whom he liked. At one stage an arrangement was mooted for the Tsar's asylum in Britain. However, probably wisely, George V was worried about the possible impact in Britain on those on the left of politics and, finally, the Government asked the French if they would grant asylum to the Tsarist family. The French agreed, but by that time it was too late. The Tsar was under arrest.

In retrospect it was indeed remarkable that virtually all political parties in Russia including even the Bolsheviks, were initially in favour of a continuation of the war. It was not until Lenin returned to Russia in April 1917 that the Bolsheviks began to call for an end to the war. The Russians were holding half of the entire force of the central powers on the Eastern Front. More Russian soldiers had been killed or had died of wounds than all the dead of all the other Allied armies put together. There was a complete breakdown of supplies, discipline and organization of every kind. There was very little government in vast areas of Russia. But still many Russians did not wish to concede victory to the Germans. The Russian Army was enormous. Before it mobilized it was 1,423,000 strong. By the end of 1914 it was 6,553,000. The total Russian casualties by the end of 1916 were 5,250,000 men. Their enthusiasm and bravery had been magnificent. But their system of supply was chaotic and they were, on the whole, extremely badly led. They were very short of NCOs – the percentage of NCOs to privates was a quarter of that in the German Army. Only one in ten officers were regular and the vast majority of officers were of peasant origin with little training.

One of the first repercussions of the new regime was known as Order Number One. It had a devastating effect on the effectiveness of the Army. It was in fact an order of the Executive Committee of the St Petersburg Soviet to the garrison of the city, but it soon spread throughout the Army. It stated that all military and naval forces should elect their own soviets (committees) and that these should send representatives to the St Petersburg Soviet which would have the ultimate power. Furthermore, soldiers should no longer have to salute their officers. This order effectively destroyed the command structure and, thereafter, it was virtually impossible to continue effective operations. (It is interesting that Trotsky, in creating the Red Army later, reversed nearly all the items of this order, including the abolition of the death penalty, which had been ordered by the Provisional Government.)

From its inception the new Government was beset by problems of every conceivable kind. The greatest was, of course, the prosecution of the war. The German High Command, too, was divided on its reaction to the Revolution. There were those who thought that they should undertake a general offensive to drive Russia out of the war once and for all, to seize the whole of the Ukraine with its vast resources, join up with Turkey, seize the Baku oil and threaten India. Others believed that if the 3,000,000 troops on the Eastern Front could immediately be transferred to the West this might well lead to the defeat of at least France before the Americans had arrived. As a result of this, the Germans dithered for a bit – but the Russians were facing a far more difficult situation. Their Prime Minister, Prince Lvov, fell before long and the new Prime Minister, Kerensky, ordered an attack. After an initial success this operation led to even further collapse and the situation became desperate. The Allies continued to attempt to shore up the Russian regime with a massive influx of arms through Archangel in the north and Vladivostok in the east, together with large loans. But it was all to little avail.

A further problem related to the inviolability of the Russian frontiers – a problem which was to recur throughout the period of the Civil War. None of the parties in Russia wished to preside over the dissolution of the Russian Empire but many of the separate nationalities on the periphery of the Russian state were pressing for independence. The right to independence for Poland and Finland were conceded, but the Provisional Government did not agree to independence for the Baltic States or any of the others.

In April 1917, as Winston Churchill put it in a typically arresting phrase, the Germans, 'transported Lenin in a sealed truck like a plague bacillus from Switzerland into Russia'. Lenin's arrival had a galvanizing effect and, together with Trotsky, who arrived later, he managed to dominate the Bolshevik Party which up to that moment had been somewhat ineffectual.

A general, Kornilov, tried to bring about a counter-revolution by marching on Petrograd, but this failed largely because of the power of the Soviets. Although Kerensky had not in fact supported this action, he became associated with it in many people's minds and his position was greatly eroded. After a series of dramatic events in Petrograd, and some hesitation by the Soviets, the second Revolution took place. On 7 November 1917 the Bolsheviks took power and Kerensky fled.[2]

It is important to remember that Lenin saw the Revolution in Russia as only the first step in what he believed would be a world revolution. On gaining power his first action at the All Russian Congress of Soviets was to promulgate the Decree of Peace. Russia would propose a general peace based on 'no annexations and no indemnities'. He expected this to precipitate an immediate revolt by the workers in all belligerent countries leading to world socialist government. In the early days of Bolshevik power in Russia all Lenin's and Trotsky's actions were to be seen in this context.

The Allies, on the other hand, were hoping against hope either that the Bolsheviks would continue the war or, if they would not do so, that they would be overthrown by some other Russian Government which would continue to fight. The arguments within and between the Allied Governments immediately after the Revolution were almost exclusively concerned with this matter.

So, in practice, both the Bolsheviks and the Allies were basing their policies on total wishful thinking: there was no question of world revolution at that moment, neither was there any likelihood that the Bolshevik Government would continue the war in any shape or form.

In fact, the second Revolution succeeded largely because the Kerensky Government did not take the decision to make peace with the Germans. It was war weariness as much and more than any other factor which brought about support for the only party which openly campaigned for an end to the fighting. The Russian people had never been so much in control of their own destiny as they were for a very short period just before the second Revolution. In fact the liberals had won the great struggle against autocracy or certainly were well on the way to doing so. As Louis de Robien, a French diplomat in Petrograd, put it in his diary on 30 April 1918:

The Russian Revolution is not the revolution of the intellectual demanding freedom of thought, of the peasant wanting land, of the workman rising against the employer, of a nation whose patience is exhausted by the excesses of a regime . . . it is simply the revolution of the soldier who does not want to go on fighting . . . The truth about the Revolution and its aims was spoken during one of last year's offensives by the soldier whose answer to Kerensky's cry of "Forward for land and liberty!" was "What use are land and liberty to me if I am killed? Peace comes first."[3]

The peasants were, of course, as are all peasants everywhere, interested in land ownership. But by the time of the second Revolution three-quarters of the land was already owned by the peasants and the last thing they wanted was a reversion to the status quo which they feared would be the result of a successful counter-revolution. In fact, of course, as they would later discover, the Bolsheviks believed in collective, not individual, ownership, and of course some of the worst excesses of Stalinism concerned the vicious attacks on peasant ownership of land.

The Bolshevik accession to power was not, therefore, a function of the disastrous nature of the Tsarist regime and its replacement by a Marxist Utopia but of the conscious decision by the Tsar's successors to continue a war which was in fact already lost as far as Russia was concerned.

In retrospect it is astonishing how long it took for the Russian ship of state to change course and, indeed, it could well be argued that it did not change course at all as one autocracy succeeded another. Habits of thought and behaviour sustained by centuries of history are not to be eradicated at a stroke. Although, of course, the urban proletariat and, to a lesser extent, the rural peasantry appear to have rejected the whole hierarchy of aristocratic rule, they did not reject the concept of autocracy – or if some of them did so they were unable to sustain their position. Furthermore, it took quite a long time for the fact of revolution to sink in. Even during the Revolution itself in Petrograd the theatres were still running and there were dances and parties in the houses of the mighty. Louis de Robien in his diary of 5

31

December 1917, a month after the second Revolution, writes of the situation in Petrograd how 'Things are going from bad to worse. The Bolsheviks have acquired the mentality of autocrats and are mercilessly breaking down all resistance . . . And during all this time, the theatres of Petrograd are full and I found it impossible to get a seat for the ballet tonight, when they are doing Eros, La Nuit d'Egypte, and Islamet.'[4]

And, Moscow, 15 June 1918: 'A very full day but a very interesting one. I spent the whole morning at the Tretyakov Gallery with Princess Gorchakov and Lazarev.'

The mainspring of the Bolshevik success undoubtedly came from the two colossi of Russian Bolshevism – Lenin and Trotsky. Without Lenin it must be doubtful if the Bolshevik Revolution would have happened in the first place: without Trotsky it must be very doubtful that it would have been able to survive.

On attaining power the first two acts of the Bolsheviks were immediately to open peace negotiations with the Germans (14 December 1917) and, secondly, to dissolve the Constituent Assembly (18 January 1918) in which the Bolsheviks had a minority of members – 168 out of 703. The factories were handed over to the workers, private trade was abolished, banks were closed and all land was transferred into public property. The whole machinery of Government as it had existed in the past was abolished. The result of all this was almost immediately to bring about starvation. The hoped for Utopian Government was very quickly replaced by direction of labour and state control of virtually all activity.

The Allied reaction to all this was one of almost total horror. The immediate fear was that the Bolsheviks, by reneging on the Treaty of London under which separate peaces were renounced by all the main Allied Governments, would enable the millions of German soldiers on the Eastern Front to move to the West and thus bring about a German victory. This had of course been almost an Allied obsession during the time of the Provisional Government and the advent to power of the Bolsheviks confirmed their worst fears. Any straw was grasped at whereby the Russians, of whatever political hue, might still somehow keep German forces deployed in the East and prevent the Central

Powers getting their hands on the vast resources of the Ukraine, Baku oil and the millions of tons of war material which the Allies, and particularly the British, had stockpiled for the Russians at Archangel and Vladivostok.

The Bolsheviks, however, went ahead with the peace process. There was dissension between Trotsky, who led the Bolshevik delegation at Brest-Litovsk where the negotiation took place, and who at one stage withdrew from the talks because of the stringency of the German demands, and Lenin, who was determined to settle for peace at virtually any price. Trotsky evolved the strange doctrine of 'No peace, no war', but the Germans merely continued their advance. Lenin managed to persuade his colleagues to agree to the German demands and the Treaty of Brest-Litovsk was signed on 3 March 1918. By that time Lenin was beginning to doubt that there would be an immediate revolution in the West: he foresaw the possibility of civil war in Russia and had begun to appreciate the vastness of the problems which faced the Bolshevik Government in Russia. He wished to free his hands of complications in the West in order to deal with these problems. By the Treaty, Lenin agreed to the loss of the Ukraine, Finland and all the Baltic provinces. Russia also had to demobilize her Army. She lost over 1,000,000 square miles, a third of her population, a third of her cultivated land and half her industry.

There were now some doubts as to whether the Russian Congress of Soviets would ratify the Treaty. Bruce Lockhart, a remarkable young man who had been a British Vice-Consul, but who, since official recognition was not forthcoming, had been promoted to become the British unofficial contact with the Soviet Government, tried to prevent ratification, as did the American equivalent, Robbins (of the Red Cross). But on 16 March 1918 Lenin's oratory won the day against the odds and the Treaty was ratified. The Germans occupied the Ukraine, signing a Treaty there with a puppet Government.

In this situation the Russian Empire began to disintegrate. Civil War was raging in Finland, which had declared its independence of Russia. The Whites, under an erstwhile Tsarist General, Mannerheim, who was to play a notable part in

Finland's later history, had been helped by the Germans, although Mannerheim remained robustly independent of them. They defeated the Reds. Finland having therefore defected from the Russian Empire, the Finnish frontier was very close to Petrograd and there were grave fears for the safety of Murmansk in the north. The Allies were extremely worried about this for two reasons: first, a German naval occupation of Murmansk and Archangel would enable their submarines to operate in the North Sea without having to pass through the Allied blockade. This would be an extremely dangerous development. Secondly, the Germans would be able to get hold of the massive supplies which the Allies had dumped at Archangel for the Russians.

There were a number of other centres of resistance to the Bolsheviks – in the Ukraine, on the Don, on the Volga, in Siberia, in the Caucasus, in Transcaspia and in the Far East. It was at this point that the lack of a coherent and coordinated policy by the Allies first became glaringly obvious. At the same time as Bruce Lockhart was trying to establish good relations with the Soviet Government through its Commissar for Foreign Affairs, Trotsky, and indeed to get it to accept Allied intervention so that the war against the Germans could continue to be prosecuted, other British agents of one kind and another were supporting a motley array of anti-Bolshevik organizations which were springing up all over the place.

Furthermore, the British Government was hopelessly divided within itself. Lloyd George felt in his bones that Britain should try to come to some kind of accommodation with the Bolsheviks and he tended to agree with Bruce Lockhart's ideas. He put his views very clearly at a later meeting of the Imperial War Cabinet on 31 December 1918: 'For Russia to emancipate herself from Bolshevism would be a redemption, but the attempt to emancipate her by foreign armies might prove a disaster to Europe as well as to Russia. The one thing to spread Bolshevism was to attempt to suppress it. To send our soldiers to shoot down the Bolsheviks would be to create Bolsheviks here. The best thing was to let Bolshevism fail of itself and act as a deterrent to the world.'[5]

Balfour, the Foreign Secretary, sat on the fence and argued

elegantly on both sides – sometimes simultaneously. Lord Robert Cecil, Balfour's Deputy, who seemed to have a far more important role that his post would normally have justified, took a position of total opposition to the Bolsheviks, as did the Chief of the Imperial General Staff, Wilson, whose views were massively reinforced when Winston Churchill became Secretary of State for War on 19 December 1918. His tone was very different to that of his Prime Minister. In a speech to his constituents at Dundee on 26 November he had said,

> *Russia is rapidly being reduced by the Bolsheviks to an animal form of barbarism. The cost of living has multiplied thirty-seven times. The paper money will not buy food or necessaries. Civil war is proceeding in all directions. The Bolsheviks maintain themselves by bloody and wholesale butcheries and murders, carried out to a large extent by Chinese executioners and armoured cars. Work of all kinds is at a standstill. The peasants are hoarding their grain. The towns and cities only keep themselves alive by pillaging the surrounding country. We must expect that enormous numbers (probably more than we have lost in the whole war) will die of starvation this winter. Civilization is being completely extinguished over gigantic areas, while Bolsheviks hop and caper like troops of ferocious baboons amid the ruins of cities and the corpses of their victims.*[6]

The French, under Clemenceau, were, naturally enough, at that stage obsessed with the necessity of preventing any further German troops being transferred to the West and, as a result, were determined to support the anti-Bolsheviks who, if they succeeded, would probably try to continue the war against Germany. The Americans, who had just entered the war, were influenced by a belief that the Bolsheviks might well not be as bad as they had been painted and that they ought to be given a chance.

In these circumstances it was no wonder that the Allied response to the Revolution and the Treaty of Brest-Litovsk was hesitant and uncertain.

With the Armistice of 11 November 1918 all pretence that the Allied intervention in Russia was connected with the war against

Germany and its allies vanished. However, without any formal declaration the purpose of the Allied intervention thereafter gradually underwent a sea-change to support for any anti-Bolshevik force which looked as if it might succeed in ousting the hated Bolsheviks from power and in restoring some kind of order in the country, although the nature of that order was never clearly agreed. To a certain extent this support took the form of training anti-Bolshevik forces in the hope that, eventually, they would be entirely self-supporting and in supplying large quantities of arms.

The Peace Conference at Versailles, which opened in January 1919, had an awe-inspiring task. It had to settle the terms for Germany and the other belligerent powers, it had to delineate the boundaries of the whole of Europe and it had to make provision for the future peace of the world. On top of all that, it had to attempt to deal with the situation in Russia which was verging on total chaos and it had to try to evolve a coherent philosophy not only in its approach to the problems of the Central Powers but also to those of the Bolshevik Government in Russia which aimed to overturn the whole pattern of behaviour within and between states which had existed for centuries. It was inconceivable that a lasting peace in Europe could be contrived unless a peaceful settlement could be achieved in Russia and its environs. Not only were the Russians not represented at the Peace Conference but there was considerable doubt as to what constituted Russia. Certainly Finland and Poland, which had been part of the Russian Empire in 1914, did not, but how about the Baltic States, the Ukraine and all the separatist and nationalistic elements of the old imperial Russia in the south who were then struggling for independence, some of which were receiving Allied help in arms, money and even in troops?

At the beginning of 1919 it looked very likely that the Bolshevist regime might collapse anyway. As we shall see, in the north the British, with their Allies, including the Americans, were in a strong position on the Murmansk railway and south of Archangel, the White Finns were close to Petrograd, Admiral Kolchak controlled Siberia, the Czechs held most of the Trans-Siberian railway, Denikin was in control of much of

36

the Caucasus, the French had landed at Odessa, and Latvia, Lithuania and Estonia, which had been under German control, were fighting for independence. If the Bolsheviks were about to collapse it seemed to the peacemakers that there was not much point in consulting them about the future shape of Europe even if statesmen assembled in Paris were prepared to deal with a body of men which many of them saw as a bunch of blood-stained murderers with no respect for the normal civilized dealings of state with state. And what would replace the Bolshevik regime? Nobody could possibly tell. There was every argument therefore for not doing anything very much about Russia. But if Russia was to be left alone as far as the making of decisions about Eastern Europe was concerned, how about the various Allied forces which were intervening in her affairs? Should they continue to intervene? To what purpose? Above all should the victorious powers aim at a resurrection of Imperial Russia, largely within her previous borders, or should they support independence for anyone who wanted it?

Even though the Germans had been defeated in 1918, there was a fear that Germany might retrieve the disaster by domi-nating a recumbent Russia. The Armistice stipulated that German forces were to remain in situ in the East until the Allies decided that it was safe for them to return to Germany and there were fears that when it came to the point they would not do so. As we shall see, there were great difficulties in getting General von der Goltz to withdraw from the Baltic states. In 1919 the French wished to establish a *cordon sanitaire* stretching from Finland in the north, through the Baltic states and Poland down to the Ukraine and Rumania in the south and there was talk of a Franco-Polish axis guaranteeing the Polish frontiers, which were greatly in dispute.

Except for the Americans, the Allies were in a state of total exhaustion at the end of the war. A generation of young men had been slaughtered. There was starvation in much of central Europe. It was hoped and expected that peace would lead to the rebuilding of shattered lives and the restoration of plenty. Certainly, virtually no one in the Allied armies wished to continue to fight. 'Demob now' was the cry. It was indeed remarkable that there were not more mutinies by the troops who found themselves involved in Russia. Some of the Americans and the British at Archangel did indeed mutiny, and the French Navy mutinied in the south. There was considerable feeling in some quarters in Britain that any war against the Bolsheviks in Russia was morally wrong, an attempt to defeat what was to many people a long-overdue revolution against a tyrannical regime. Indeed there was a mutiny in Folkestone in January 1919 at which banners were carried which proclaimed, 'We will not fight in Russia'. It was not surprising, therefore, that there was no great enthusiasm for massive intervention by most of the participants of the Versailles negotiations. Winston Churchill and Marshal Foch did often press for a great military effort, but they did not succeed in persuading their superiors to agree.

President Wilson succeeded in capturing the imagination of much of Europe with his idealistic approach to the peace. Such was the appeal of his Fourteen Points and his generally liberal view of self-determination and magnanimity towards the vanquished that the Bolsheviks at one stage were worried that he would steal their thunder. On the boat on the way over the Atlantic Wilson, in giving a pep talk to his advisers, said, 'If the Conference does not express the wishes of the people the result might be the break-up of society.' Bolshevism was gaining credence because it was a protest against the way the world had worked. The American delegation should fight for a new order based on justice. To the hardened old campaigners from Europe gathered in Paris, this no doubt sounded like the effusions of an immature schoolboy – but Wilson's words did have a fresh and invigorating tang which promised something positive. The idea of a League of Nations, too, gave a hope of continuing peace to a world on the point of collapse.

It was one of the great tragedies of world history that not only was Wilson's vision of a League of Nations, which would safeguard world peace, to fail, largely because his own country did not join it, but virtually every one of his Fourteen Points was to be circumvented and only four of Wilson's twenty-three conditions for a just peace were ever incorporated in a peace treaty.

As far as Russia was concerned Wilson was torn between two

conflicting concepts. On the one hand he felt instinctively that the Bolshevik Government had some popular legitimacy and might well succeed in its aim of bringing about a measure of prosperity and freedom. At the least it should be left alone: if the people supported it, it would succeed. If they did not, it would fail. On the other hand he was shocked by much of what he heard of the Bolshevik practice and by the rejection of all civilized relationship between states. The Bolshevik Terror had a great effect on him. He was also subjected to considerable pressures by those around him. In some ways Wilson's views were similar to Lloyd George's. The latter, too, thought that the Bolsheviks might well succeed and that they could well have a measure of popular support. But where Wilson was somewhat naive in political matters, Lloyd George was the consummate politician, ready to twist and turn, to modify and even to reverse his views in accordance with the current climate. He was a master of intrigue and double-dealing. His views of the morality and advisability of intervention changed according to whether the Bolsheviks were doing well or badly. When they were doing well, he was adamantly opposed to any action at all: when they were doing badly he was all in favour of supporting their enemies to the hilt.

Apart from Clemenceau, whose whole approach was conditioned by the necessity of preventing the Germans of ever being in a position to renew their threat to France and of obtaining from them the maximum reparations in order to rebuild his shattered country, the other major figure at the Peace Conference was Winston Churchill. He was all in favour of massive intervention and supporting the anti-Bolshevist forces to the maximum. He was certain that Bolshevism could be defeated by military force and that it was only weakness of character which prevented the Allies from strangling this monster at birth.

One of the major problems which faced the Allies at Versailles was that of Russian representation. If the question of the establishment of a whole battery of new countries in the east – Latvia, Lithuania, Estonia, Finland, the Ukraine, Georgia, Azerbaijan, and so on – was to be discussed, let alone decided, then surely the Russians themselves should be represented and both Lloyd George and Wilson argued eloquently to that effect. But who was to represent Russia? The Bolsheviks whose aim was the collapse of the whole order of nation states and who were certainly not in control of the majority of the old Tsarist Russia? Or representatives of the old order – Kerensky, who had escaped from Russia and certainly had virtually no support left even among the émigrés? How about representatives of the old Tsarist regime? There were plenty of them around arguing that they alone had legitimacy. Or perhaps one of the three major anti-Bolshevik regimes operating in Russia – Tchaikovsky in the north, Denikin in the south or Kolchak in the east. And if so, which one? Or perhaps a combination of two or more of those claimants, if they could agree to submerging their difficulties.[7]

On the other hand it might be better to shelve the whole issue and to leave the whole matter of a settlement of the Russian problem to subsequent negotiations. But some problems which impinged on Russian sovereignty had to be settled immediately: the Baltic States still had German troops deployed on their soil; the Germans were still in control of much of the Ukraine and so on.

Wilson and Lloyd George pressed for a conference to be held in Paris with invitations to be sent to all the anti-Bolshevik factions in Russia and to the Bolsheviks. The French objected strongly and made suggestions for an all-out attack on the Soviet Union, to be carried out, apparently, with American and Polish troops. This was rejected out of hand by the Americans and the eventual result was that invitations were sent to all parties in the conflict in Russia to attend a conference at the islands of Prinkipo in the Sea of Marmora close to Constantinople.

The invitations were not sent as such to the potential partici-pants but were published as an open invitation. The Soviet Government accepted the invitation while making a number of concessions, but with qualifications. The various anti-Bolshevik Russian leaders rejected the invitation. In general, they were appalled that they were being asked to sit down with their murderous enemies, the Bolsheviks.

The whole exercise is a tragic example of the difficulties of achieving a common approach to a complex and difficult issue when the basic aims of those attempting to agree on a policy differ widely.

Moreover, the disagreements were not only between participating nations, but within national delegations. In an extraordinary series of incidents in February 1919, Lloyd George and Winston Churchill were putting forward diametrically opposite policies and later Balfour, the Foreign Secretary, was openly attacking Churchill's proposals for massive intervention at a meeting of the Council of Ten of the Conference. Later still, Philip Kerr, Lloyd George's Private Secretary, was briefing the Americans that his boss disagreed profoundly with the views of Winston Churchill who was representing Britain at the Conference at the time.

The next attempts to secure some kind of accommodation with Soviet Russia took place when Bullitt, a very junior (28 years old) member of the American delegation to Versailles was sent to Moscow by Colonel House, the American head of the delegation at Versailles, with the approval of President Wilson, who had returned to the United States. The original idea of the mission was that it would be fact-finding only, but later, probably at the instigation of Bullitt himself[8], it developed into an attempt to establish by negotiation whether the Soviets would be prepared to make sufficient concessions for the Americans, and perhaps the Allies too, to establish economic relations with them, distribute food and other aid and generally come to an accommodation. The Soviets were prepared to make considerable concessions including 'The retention by all de facto Governments in Russia of control of the territories they occupied until the conference [a peace conference was to be set up in a neutral country] decided on territorial changes or the peoples therein determined to change their Government'. The Soviets also agreed to be responsible for Russia's debts.

The terms, certainly, constituted a basis for negotiations which had many advantages for the Allies.

In the event the Bullitt proposals never came to anything. This was partly because the American President was too tired and exhausted to concentrate on more than one matter at a time and he was in the middle of a major confrontation with

Clemenceau about the German Peace Treaty. But it was also because the ideas were leaked to the press and Lord Northcliffe's newspapers mounted a major attack on the 'secret intrigue' with Bolshevism' arousing conservative opinion in Britain and the United States which was violently opposed to any question of dealing with the Bolsheviks. Lloyd George became alarmed at the possible damage to his coalition and distanced himself from the Bullitt mission, even going so far as to deny knowledge of it, whereas, in fact, of course he had been fully informed about the whole affair by his Private Secretary, Philip Kerr, who had even gone so far as to draft possible terms of the peace accommodation himself. Of all the instances of Lloyd George's double dealing this is perhaps one of the most flagrant.

Meanwhile Marshal Foch had been proposing ever more grandiose schemes of military intervention advocating a general attack on Bolshevism by anyone he could think of – Poles, Rumanians, Russians, Czechs, French, Americans, British and so on. These were all turned down by President Wilson and Lloyd George and even Clemenceau began to become a bit embarrassed by his military adviser's activities.

Allied policy towards Russia, fragmented and uncertain as it was during the deliberations on the Peace Treaty at Versailles, did at least have the benefit of a common forum for the Allied leaders as long as these deliberations continued. Wilson, Lloyd George, Clemenceau and Orlando, the Prime Minister of Italy, did occasionally discuss the Russian question and sometimes even came to some kind of conclusion.

However, after the Peace Treaty was signed in June 1919 the Allied leaders never went to Paris again as a body and any semblance of a common policy vanished.

The following chapters will examine what actually happened.

Chapter Three

THE NORTH

A British naval presence was established in North Russia early in the war in order to counter the German submarine threat to the northern sea lanes. During the summer, when the White Sea was not frozen, the ships were based at Archangel, the Russian town and port at the south-east corner of the White Sea, whence a railway ran through Vologda to Moscow. As the war continued, very large quantities of military equipment were shipped to Archangel for onward transmission to the Russian armies fighting the Germans. During the winter, from November to May, the small British fleet moved to Murmansk on the Kola Inlet from the Barents Sea, an ice-free port built by the Russians during the war in order to provide the Allies with continued access to Russia. Considerable military supplies for the Russian armies were sent to Murmansk in the winter. The Russians, with immense effort, also constructed a single track railway from Murmansk to Petrograd. Both the port and the railway were finished at the end of 1916. The British Admiral, Kemp, and his staff, however, remained in Archangel during the winter of 1916.

After the second, Bolshevik, Revolution in November 1917, due to worries about their safety, the British Admiral and his staff moved to Murmansk. In fact, the Governor General of Archangel retained his position for a few months after the Revolution before being superseded by a coalition of anti-Bolshevik Socialists. In late January 1918 a Bolshevik 'Extraordinary Commission' arrived in the town and began to move the military stores into the interior for use by the Bolshevik military forces.[1]

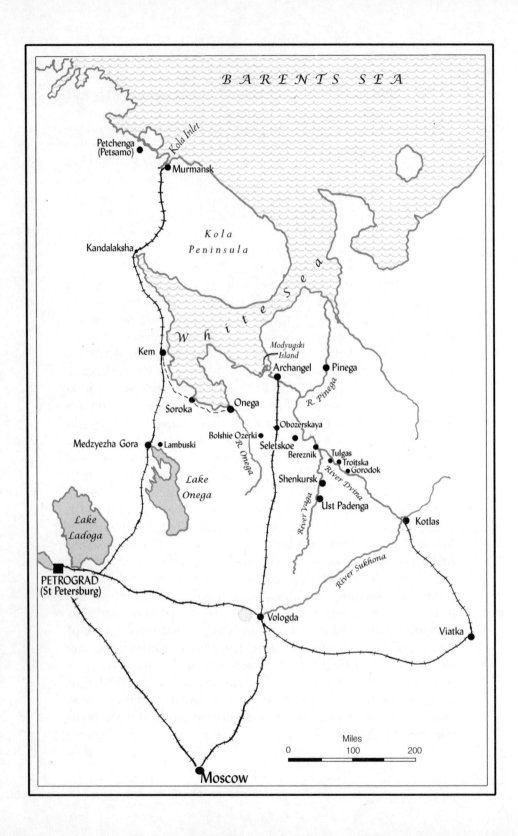

While Admiral Kemp remained in Murmansk with his battle-ship *Glory* and a few minesweepers, the town (if it can be described as such) came under the control of a Soviet – a council of workers. Also in the port were several Russian ships including a battleship, a cruiser and four destroyers. As elsewhere, the Russian sailors were among the most extreme Bolshevik supporters. They took over the ships from their officers and constituted an imminent threat to the British naval presence. On top of this, there were fears of a German attack through Finland in conjunction with the White Finns who, under General Mannerheim, were fighting a civil war against the Red Finns who had taken the reins of power throughout the country. In fact, the German threat was largely imaginary. It was caused by the fact that the White Finns were using German equipment and had a few German officers serving with them. However, the Murmansk Soviet was extremely worried and it telegraphed Trotsky to ask if it could accept assistance from the British. At that moment it looked as if the peace negotiations at Brest-Litovsk between the Bolsheviks and the Germans were on the point of failure and Trotsky was afraid that the Germans would resume their advance. As a result, he told the Murmansk Soviet to 'accept any and all assistance from the Allied missions'. And so Allied intervention in Russia started on 6 March 1918 when a company of marines was landed at Murmansk from HMS *Glory* and went into barracks on shore.

There was very little that such a small force could accomplish, but, as almost always appears to be the case with similar initial small incursions, this was the precursor of many thousands of British and other troops in the north, east and south of Russia, who very shortly found themselves fighting against the Bolsheviks whom they had originally landed to support, together with a naval squadron in the Baltic which sank a number of Bolshevik ships. [There are similarities here to the military inter-vention in Northern Ireland which, originally, took place in order to protect the Catholics against the Protestants.] Admiral Kemp asked for an Allied expeditionary force of at least 6,000 men in order to protect the British base. No troops were avail-able, but the British and French each sent a cruiser and later the

Americans followed suit, the American cruiser *Olympia* arriving in Murmansk carrying the British Major General Poole who assumed command of all the Allied troops in North Russia.

After his initial reaction to the Murmansk Soviet's telegram, Trotsky, with the support of Lenin, changed his mind. He was worried that the Germans would see the Allied military presence in Murmansk as a clear breach of the Treaty of Brest-Litovsk of 3 March 1918, which in fact it was, and would resume their advance, capture Petrograd and oust the Bolshevik Government. He therefore instructed the Murmansk Soviet to cease any co-operation with the Allied forces and to demand their instant withdrawal. The Murmansk Soviet, however, refused to obey these orders and was, therefore, in direct conflict with the Soviet Government.

On 23 June 1918 the British sent a further 600 infantry and a machine-gun company together with a mission of seven officers and 500 other ranks intended to go to Archangel to help the creation of an anti-Bolshevik Russian force prepared to continue the war against Germany and to equip and train such Czechoslovak forces as might arrive there from Siberia.

Major-General Maynard arrived with the British reinforcements in order to take command of the Murmansk Front under the overall command of Major-General Poole who was to control affairs from Archangel where the Bolsheviks were in nominal control, although the situation there was, to say the least, confused.

Before Maynard's arrival a Serbian battalion had appeared on the scene. Very many of them were sick, however, and they were of little practical use at that stage. Some local Russians and some Poles had been enlisted and were in the process of being trained and equipped. There were also some '500 scurvy-ridden Red Finns who had been driven out of their country by the Whites'. Their tendencies were probably Bolshevik. They would certainly be ready to oppose the White Finns and perhaps, the Germans. They had been enlisted in a Finn Legion.

Before Maynard's arrival Poole had established a military presence of a kind at Kandalashka and Kem on the railway south of Murmansk and a small landing party at Petchenga (Petsamo) on the Barents Sea north-west of Murmansk. The position on Maynard's arrival was, therefore, as follows:-

Murmansk: 150 Royal Marines, 400 Serbians (nearly all sick), 150 Russians and Poles (just enlisted)

Kandalashka: French artillery group (ill-equipped and many sick), Serbian battalion (many unfit), Finn Legion

Kem: 250 Royal Marines, 250 of the Serbian battalion

Petchenga: 150 landing party from HMS Cochrane *(a cruiser)*[2]

In his diary Commander Drage gives a vivid account of his time at Petchenga commanding an extraordinary mixture of British sailors, French soldiers, Red Guards and Red sailors, skirmishing against the White Finns. He added, 'July 20 1918. They are a mixed crowd here. The star turn is a Chinaman who is reported to have attacked two girls, killed them and eaten them . . . We had the inter-squadron shooting match today . . . duck shooting and fishing almost every day.'[3] Life in northern Russia at that time was certainly nothing if not varied.

There were said to be, and this was probably the case, two Red Guard Bolshevik Divisions to the south of Murmansk. It was not immediately clear what their intentions as regards the Allies were, but Maynard clearly had to attempt to prevent their advancing along the railway line towards Murmansk. By a mixture of bluff and the occasional show of force, by mid-July 1918 he managed to secure the railway as far south as Soroka where the track to Archangel veered off to the east. He was greatly helped by having complete control of the White Sea, from which he was able to bring his naval guns to bear when required and to ferry supplies to his various garrisons. Later (on 21 May 1919) Maynard's forces captured Medvyezha Gora on the shore of Lake Onega.

Poole, who later came under considerable criticism for his imperious manner and his tactless handling of the anti-Bolshevik Russian hierarchy, showed considerable powers of leadership and readiness to take risks when on 1 August 1918 he succeeded in capturing Archangel from the Bolsheviks who were, by then, sending south a considerable tonnage of war supplies each day. The port had been ice-bound until mid-July and Poole was very short of troops to make a landing. A French colonial infantry battalion had arrived at Murmansk on 26 July and Poole decided to attack. His naval support consisted of the British cruiser *Attentive* and the aircraft carrier *Nairene*, together with the French cruiser *Admiral Abe*. This latter ship struck a submerged wreck and did not appear on the scene until the affray was over. However, *Nairene's* seaplanes and *Attentive's* guns silenced the Bolshevik batteries at Modyugski, an island fort guarding the Archangel channel and no further opposition was met. The Bolsheviks quickly evacuated Archangel.

After a meeting between Kemp and the very Russian, in spite of his name, young naval Captain, Chaplin, an anti-Bolshevik coup in Archangel had been organized to coincide with the attack. This was entirely successful and a pro-Ally, anti-Bolshevik Government was installed under the veteran Socialist leader Nicholas Tchaikovsky who had spent twenty-six years of exile in England and six in the United States where he had tried, but failed, to found a religious cult. As a result of his years in England and America he spoke English fluently, which was a great advantage in his dealings with the many non-Russian speaking Allied officers with whom he had to deal. His Government was strong on speeches, the passing of resolutions and interminable meetings about very little, but weak on the initiation of action of any kind. He was also, as a Socialist, opposed to the many ex-Tsarist officers who had gathered in Archangel, including Captain Chaplin who, shortly after the first coup, organized another in which the entire Government was arrested and transported to an island in the White Sea. This was too much for the Allies. Tchaikovsky and his Government were reinstated and Chaplin was arrested. A few months later he was discovered by General Ironside sitting alone in a tent singing mournful Russian songs to himself accompanied by his balalaika.

The Bolsheviks retreated quickly to the south down the

railway and the River Dvina. Poole organized follow-up parties of mixed nationalities – British, French, Russian and Poles. On the railway a train was used; on the river the party travelled in three steamers.[4] At first there was little opposition from the Bolsheviks but eventually this stiffened, particularly on the river where the Bolsheviks had four gunboats. The Allies eventually brought up a monitor and two gunboats which succeeded in pushing the Bolsheviks further back. By the end of August 1918 Allied columns were established on the railway and river 100 and 120 miles respectively south of Archangel.

The difficulties inherent in any force composed of mixed nationalities were already beginning to be felt. In his diary M.N.G. Watson (later Brigadier) who was acting as supply officer to the Allied forces remarks, 'French marines were sent up the line on the railway but they were a nuisance as every ten days they had to be taken out of the line and sent down to base so that they could visit their women.'[5] He clearly believed this rather unlikely story. Racial prejudice was not confined to the British, however, as Watson added, 'The Jews were equally hated by both sides of Russians. It did not matter which side captured them. They were put to death in a brutal matter.' There was much prejudice, too, in what the British soldiers were told when they arrived in Russia. In his papers J.H. Bracher produced the following 'proclamation' (presumably written by the local military authority) which was issued to British troops on arrival purporting to explain why they were there:

> There seems to be among the troops a very indistinct idea of what we were fighting for here in North Russia. This can be explained in a few words. We are up against Bolshevism, which means anarchy pure and simple. Any one of you can understand that no State can possibly exist when its own internal affairs, such as labour, railways, relations with Foreign Powers etc are so disorganized as to make life impossible for everybody. Look at Russia at the present moment. The power is in the hands of a few men, mostly Jews (sic), who have succeeded in bringing the country to such a state that order is nonexistent, the posts and railways do not run properly, every man who wants something

that somebody else has got, just kills his opponent, only to be killed himself when the next man comes along. Human life is not safe, you can buy justice at so much for each object. Prices of necessities have so risen that nothing is procurable. In fact the man with the gun is "cock of the walk" provided that he does not meet another man who is a better shot. The result is that the country as a whole suffers and becomes the prey of any adventurers who happen along. Bolshevism is a disease which, like consumption, kills its victim and brings no good to anybody. Undoubtedly things will be changed after the war, but not by anarchy and wholesale murder. Bolshevism to start with was only commenced with the sanction of Germany to rid the latter of a dangerous enemy, Russia. Now, Bolshevism has grown upon the uneducated masses to such an extent that Russia is disintegrated and helpless and therefore we have come to help her to get rid of the disease that is eating her up. We are not here to conquer Russia, and none of us want to stay here but we want to help her and see her as a great power, as at present she is lying helpless in the hands of the adventurers who are simply exploiting her for their own ends and who, in order to attain their ends, kill off their opponents from the highest to the lowest, including those who have the best brains in the country, whose powers could be used to restore her prestige and place among the nations. When order is restored here we shall clear out, but only when we have obtained our object and that is the restoration of Russia.[6]

Even if this description of the situation in Russia was wholly true, which it certainly was not, it is difficult to imagine any instruction to soldiers which was quite so contrary to what their political masters intended. It is true that Churchill, the Minister for War, had been uttering very bellicose noises about Bolshevism and the situation in Russia. But his views were not shared by the rest of the Cabinet. In particular, the Prime Minister, Lloyd George's views were very, almost diametrically, different, and the British were in North Russia as the result of decisions taken by the Cabinet and its Prime Minister. Lloyd George's consistent views were summed up in a telegram he sent Churchill during the long-running argument he was having with his subordinate Minister of War:

If Russia is really anti-Bolshevik, then a supply of equipment would enable it to redeem itself. If Russia is now Bolshevik, not merely is it none of our business to interfere with its internal affairs, it would be positively mischievous: it would strengthen and consolidate Bolshevik opinion. An expensive war of aggression against Russia is a way to strengthen the Bolsheviks in Russia and create it at home.[7]

To return to the battlefront, the comparative ease of the operations in North Russia in their early stages had led to a completely false estimation of the military potentialities of the Bolshevik armies. As General Finlayson (Poole's deputy), who was in effective command of the operations south of Archangel, later noted:

The Bolsheviks were mistakenly dismissed as a great rabble of men armed with sticks, stones and revolvers who rush about foaming at the mouth and who are easily turned and broken by a few well-directed rifle shots.[8]

When the Bolshevik forces did fight well, a further myth was created to the effect that, because they were normally so inept, they must be led by German officers.

Indeed, yet another 'Sheet of general information of general interest to troops arriving in Russia' was issued.[9] There were two categories noted under 'the enemy'.

The Bolsheviks were described as:

. . . soldiers and sailors who, in the majority of cases are criminal. Their natural vicious brutality enabled them to assume leadership. The Bolshevik is now fighting desperately because the restoration of order means an end to his regime and, secondly, because he sees a noose around his neck for his misdeeds if he is caught . . .

As for the Germans,

The Bolsheviks have no capacity for organization but this is supplied by Germany and her lesser allies. The Germans usually appear in Russian uniform and are impossible to distinguish.

The document went on

> We are fighting Bolsheviks who are the worst form of criminals
> . . . The Bolshevik Government is entirely in the hands of the
> Germans who have backed this party against all others in Russia,
> owing to the simplicity of maintaining anarchy in a totally dis-
> organized country. Therefore, we are definitely opposed to the
> Bolshevik-cum-German party. In regard to other parties we
> express no criticism and will accept them as we find them
> provided they are fighting for "Russia" and therefore "out with
> the Boche". Briefly, we do not meddle in internal affairs.

Whatever the overall rights and wrongs of this rather extraordinary document, it is certainly wrong about German control
of Russian affairs. After the Treaty of Brest-Litovsk there was
indeed a German Ambassador in Moscow but it was ludicrous
to assert that the Government was in the hands of the Germans:
there were no Germans attached to the Russian Army.

The country in which the Allied soldiers would find themselves operating until September 1919 was very different from
what they were accustomed to in Western Europe. Maynard
described Murmansk as:

> A mere collection of log-built houses with no single building of
> brick and stone. Litter and rubbish were heaped on the foreshore
> and alongside the unkempt tracks which served as roads . . . .
> Outside many of the huts was such a conglomeration of
> unsavoury rubbish that one shrank from the very thought of ever
> being compelled to enter them. It is a region of tundra akin to
> coarse peat; and for mile after mile from Murmansk almost to the
> shores of Lake Onega there is no sign of cultivation – nothing but
> tundra and the eternal forests of pine and fir.[10]

Added to the general look of squalor was the appearance of the
inhabitants themselves. 'Many nationalities had been used to
build the railway – in addition to the Russians the population
included Poles, Koreans, Letts, Chinese and other foreigners, a
motley and unprepossessing crowd.' [A highly chauvinistic,
although at the time typical, summing-up].

Private Hirst of the Yorkshire Regiment had somewhat similar views:

People in England who grumble should just come over here and see how these people have to exist. Their houses are all wood and would not do as a pig sty for us . . . people here are having a hard life; for a packet of cigs they would give as much as twenty roubles[11]

The town of Archangel was also different from Murmansk. Although not a very old town – it had been built by Peter the Great – it boasted a fine cathedral and a number of substantial houses. It lies some twenty-five miles up the Dvina River, which at that point is about the breadth of the Thames at Westminster Bridge. It had been the centre of a very flourishing timber business and there was a proliferation of busy saw mills on the river as it flowed away from Archangel towards the White Sea. The whole countryside was covered with mile upon mile of pine trees interspersed with a marshy land and the occasional village, each of which had a priest, a church and a number of strongly built houses for the peasant population. Like all peasants everywhere they were not interested in politics and merely wished to be left alone to pursue their somewhat arduous life in peace. They would support whichever side they thought would win.

A.E. Thompson, a wireless operator, arrived in Archangel on 30 September 1918 and described it as follows:

The town is simply one long straight road, five or six miles long, with a tramway down the centre. The pavements are of wood as are all the buildings. The people are clad in every conceivable combination of cloth and fur. The women work as hard as the men and can be seen sawing huge logs. The roadways are made of huge stones . . . there is nothing on sale in the shops and I am told that the people are practically starving. Certainly the majority of people are in rags.[12]

M.G.C. Gawthorpe described Archangel as 'a dull place. Nothing to see but a few troops and sailors of all kinds and a few fat women and girls so squat as to be repulsive.'[13]

Lieutenant Tyler RN, who arrived in Archangel in HMS *Hunter*, a small monitor, much later on 9 June 1919 summed up the place as a 'filthy, dirty town whose inhabitants smelt horribly'.[14] Indeed the stench of untreated sewage was one of the principal memories of virtually all Allied soldiers that served in North Russia in 1918/19.

President Wilson had been adamantly opposed to any American intervention in Russia but had come under heavy pressure by the British Government to change his mind and, at last and against his better judgement, agreed on 17 July 1918 to American intervention in North Russia, subject to the condition that American troops could only be used 'to guard military stores which may subsequently be needed by Russian forces in the organization of their self-defence'. Crucially, however, he agreed that the Americans should come under British command. The American force sent to North Russia consisted of the 339th Infantry Regiment made up of three battalions, together with the 310th Engineer Regiment, the 377th Field Hospital and the 377th Ambulance Company – a total of 4,487 men. They all came from Michigan or Wisconsin and their training had consisted only of a month at Camp Custer followed by a second month spent crossing the Atlantic. They had expected to be sent to France. They arrived in Aldershot, England, and were fitted out with winter equipment and Russian rifles (manufactured by Westinghouse). They had little confidence in these weapons and each man had only fired ten rounds with a rifle on a range before leaving Newcastle on 26 August 1918.[15] They were commanded by Colonel George E. Stewart.

As well as trying to cope with the military problems and the near chaotic civilian situation in Archangel, with a population many of whom had Bolshevik sympathies, together with numerous ex-Tsarist officers and other hangers-on of the Tsarist regime, Poole had to deal with the many Allied Ambassadors who, having left Petrograd after the Revolution, finally arrived in Archangel from Petrograd via Vologda and Kandalashka at the western end of the White Sea. The British Minister Sir Francis Lindley was most sensible and helpful. The American Ambassador David M. Francis, a thrusting businessman much out of his depth in the intrigue-ridden maelstrom of the Russian political life of the times, was all in favour of decisive military intervention and did not demur when Poole immediately sent two of the American battalions up the line – one to Obozerskaya, seventy miles to the south on the railway and another, with a battalion of Royal Scots, in river boats up the Dvina to join the British force of naval monitors and infantry patrols there in an effort to seize Bereznik. These movements were in direct contravention of the clear orders which had been received from President Wilson which, as we have seen, were explicitly confined to the guarding of military stores.

The Americans had had a nightmarish journey out to Archangel in three vastly overcrowded transports, which were affected by the virulent Spanish influenza of the time. Three hundred and seventy-eight Americans caught the disease and no less than seventy-two died.[16]

Rarely can there have been a military force sent into action with such totally unsuitable backgrounds. The British were nearly all categorized as B or C – to be used only for guard duties – the Americans were almost totally untrained and just recovering from the ravages of influenza, and the French Colonial Battalion, who found themselves very far from home, were engaged in a struggle which they neither understood nor cared about one way or the other.

Not surprisingly, there was immediate friction between the British and the Americans, who bitterly resented coming under British command. As the American Brigadier Richardson later reported:

> It is interesting to note that the British policy has not been one, in any sense, of cooperation with the Allies, but of merely employing such forces as were obtained from the other Allies, subordinated in every way to British direction. I naturally expected upon my arrival to be taken somewhat into the confidence of the British Command as to their plans and policy, but I soon found that I was mistaken in this respect, and found a difficulty even in getting orders issued through these headquarters for the movements of American troops – it having been the practice of the British Command to ignore the Commanding Officer of

American troops, except to call upon him for support in enforcing orders issued to the troops without his knowledge or concurrence, and for action in matters of complaint against American officers and troops.

The American attitudes to the British Allies can be summed up in the headline to chapter three of the book *The Ignorant Armies – The Anglo-American Archangel Expedition* by E.M. Halliday. The headline reads 'Doughboys to the rescue'. The British found the idea of the Americans coming late on the scene to pull their chestnuts out of the fire for them intensely irritating. Similar feelings had already arisen in the first war and certainly were to arise in the second. Furthermore the British, not surprisingly in view of a total lack of military experience of the Americans, found them very naïve. Some British soldiers went much further than this in their views, 'I put the Yanks below the Bolsheviks even . . . they're a hopeless mob and as windy as hell.'[18]

For their part, the Americans were apt to blame the British for everything:

We are under British control. Mind you, the English own us; they can do with us what they please. Good God, you cannot believe how these English are hated around here. They have officers that outrank our officers. If one of our officers is promoted as high as theirs, they promote one higher again. And just think, we must do as they say and the goddamn fools are of more harm than good. They can't fight.

Would you believe it? We haven't enough men or supplies to fight with. The Bolos have better artillery than we have and they can use it also. Of course it's English doings. But think of the disgrace to the Americans who are pushed into this deed, into this dead fire by those English, and must backwater, which an American hates to do. It's hell I'm telling you.[19]

In the early stages of the campaign the British Commander-in-Chief, Ironside, who, as we shall see, superseded Poole, also found the Americans very inadequate. 'I have seen many American regiments in France and had them under my command, but I have never seen anything quite so bad as this regiment . . . the regiment has received no training and the officers were, one and all, of the lowest value imaginable . . . I do not think this regiment is fit to carry out active operations.'[20] Ironside did not have a much better opinion of the French Colonial Battalion, which he found 'in a thoroughly disaffected state'. Indeed, George Finlayson dammed them as a 'sullen band of strikers and shirkers'.

A further, unexpected and strange, complication to the relationship between the Americans and their British commanders was the fact that, apparently, many of the Americans did not speak English, coming as they did from recent immigrant communities. Major (later Brigadier) Gilmore found himself at one stage on the River Dvina with, among others, an American company under command. He said in his diary that one of his difficulties was that, 'the Americans spoke every European language bar English'.[21] However, this was not universally true about the Americans. General Ironside himself recalled how 'American ways of answering senior officers were often curious . . . when I had spoken sharply to a company commander about something his men had done, he held out his hand with the words "General I am with you". To this day I am not quite certain whether he meant to say whether he agreed with me, or merely had heard what I said.'[22]

During the first months of intervention at Archangel the Allied force consisted of 4,800 Americans, 2,420 British (including a battalion of Royal Scots), 900 French and 350 Serbs – a predominantly American force. Poole had proclaimed martial law and was interfering directly in matters which should have been left to the Tchaikovsky Government. He issued a decree that any attempt to spread 'false rumours calculated to provoke unrest or disturbance among the troops and population would be punishable by death'.[23] Maynard, on the other hand, who had much the easier task at Murmansk, both because he was not directly engaged in much fighting against the Bolsheviks – indeed, he was using some Red Finns in operations against the White Finns – and because the local Russian Soviet in Murmansk supported him, was successful in his appeals for reinforcements to counter the mythical German advance. By mid-September he had 15,000 men directly under his command. There were 7,400 British, including an infantry brigade of four battalions, two machine-gun companies, a mortar battery and a three battery brigade of field artillery. He also had 1,000 French, 1,350 Italians (who had very smart uniforms but not much else), 1,200 Serbs and more than 4,000 Russian Karelians and Finns.[24]

Poole, too, had asked for reinforcements in order to mount an offensive along the railway and the River Dvina, both in order to gather Russian recruits for the Russian anti-Bolshevik Army and in order eventually to link up with Admiral Kolchak's anti-Bolshevik Russian Army in Siberia and, as we shall see later, with some of the Czech corps which, he had been told, would push towards Archangel in order to leave for the Western Front. However, these reinforcements had been refused.

Both Maynard and Poole were having difficulties in feeding the populations for which they had assumed responsibility. Frequent and urgent requests for food had met with scant response.

On 14 October 1918 Poole had left for England in order, as he thought, to discuss the situation in North Russia with the War Office. In fact President Wilson, no less, had complained of his general attitudes and his contemptuous dealing with the US force nominally under his control, and he was replaced by General Ironside who had just arrived, in theory to act as his Chief of Staff.

Ironside was an inspired choice. As apparently so often is the case with the British military hierarchy, when morale is low and little military or political progress is being made, the British produce out of the hat a General whose personality transforms the situation. Roberts in South Africa, Allenby in Palestine in the First World War, Montgomery in the North Africa and Slim in Burma in the Second World War and Templer in Malaya in 1952 (the author was serving in Malaya at the time and felt the full force of the immediate transformation of morale when Templer arrived). The precedents are clear and remarkable.

Ironside was only thirty-seven years old when he was plucked out of France where he was commanding a brigade and thrown into the situation in North Russia, which was as precarious militarily as it was complicated politically. He was an immense man physically, about twenty stone and six foot four inches tall. He spoke Russian, French, German, Italian and Swedish and, apparently, had a smattering of eleven other languages.[25] He particularly impressed the Russians because he could curse them in their own language.[26] He had vast powers of leadership, travelling among his very split command by sleigh through the snow accompanied only by his faithful two servants Piskoff and Kostia. No one under his command was quite certain that this vast figure might not turn up at any time of the day or night. Unlike his predecessor Poole, he was extremely tactful with the White Russian commanders and politicians, and all who met him, including the very touchy Americans, were greatly impressed. Indeed, in all the records of the campaign the author has not found one comment about him which is not highly enthusiastic about his personality, good sense and ability.

Ironside realized immediately that the greatest problem with which he would have to deal would be the arctic winter which was fast approaching. The summer had brought with it not only the marshy conditions of much of the countryside as the snow melted but also the often intolerable affliction of mosquitoes which permeated that part of the world and, apparently, still do. Indeed, as the *Hampshire Regiment Journal* of July 1919 records, 'All our troops wore mosquito veils around their caps and it was understood by the anti-Bolshevik Russians that any move without them might be Bolshevik and that they could shoot on sight. One correspondent (*The Times*) who forgot his veil was fired at by machine gun and had a fortunate escape.' One totally unforeseen difficulty was that some of the troops sent to northern Russia from Mesopotamia had the malaria bug on them and some mosquitoes became infected, passing it on. Luckily this did not, in practice, prove to be a major problem.

The winter was something else. With thirty degrees of frost a common occurrence, it was clearly essential to make sure that the Allied soldiers understood about the dangers of frostbite and how to avoid it. Any metal touched in the open would lead to serious burning and any kind of wound necessitating a prolonged stay in the open was certain to lead to death. There was no continuous Front, rather a series of defence posts consisting mainly of blockhouses made of wood, warmed by the ubiquitous Russian stoves. Supply was a great problem and H.N.B. Watson (later Brigadier), who was concerned with organizing supply, states in his diary that on the River Dvina Front (the railway front was mainly supplied by train) 900 sleighs were used in relays each day.[27] This was clearly a massive organizational feat. Another problem faced by those concerned in both Archangel and Murmansk was producing the currency to pay the drivers and, indeed, in Murmansk this led to a strike. Furthermore, food had to be produced not only for the Allied soldiers but also, very often, for the local population who were only prepared to help the Allies if they were provided with food. One great advantage of the arctic winter as far as Ironside was concerned, however, was that it gave great help to the defence. Any attacker had to move across country and, provided the blockhouses had organized clear fields of fire for themselves (an immediate imperative as Ironside recognized) a stubborn defence would be very difficult, if not impossible, to overcome.

It was not long before Ironside was faced with his first major, and perhaps most difficult, problem – mutiny. As we have seen, one of the main objectives of the Allied move into North Russia had always been to raise and train enough White Russian troops so that they would be self-sufficient when the Allies left – there was never any question of a permanent garrison. There were two quite different and separate kinds of anti-Bolshevik Russian forces. First were the Slavo-British Legion, consisting of refugees and ex-Tsarist officers in the ranks with British officers. Then there were the more regular units composed mainly of conscripted peasants and others who lived in the area. The discipline of this latter force was very uncertain and the first time the first Archangel company of this latter force was ordered to parade it refused to do so. Firm action restored the situation but a nasty taste was left in the mouth and it was the precursor of other, more serious, events.

During the first few weeks after Ironside's arrival both sides were eyeing each other rather nervously, occasionally sparring for position and making the odd foray to test each others' morale and strength. This came to an end on 11 November 1918 (Armistice Day) when the Bolsheviks made a major attack on the River Dvina Front. The British gunboats had been peremptorily withdrawn because of the fear of being frozen in. However, the Bolshevik gunboats were still operating. No less than 4,000 shells fell on the Allied positions during the three days of action.[28] The Royal Scots (composed entirely of men considered unfit for anything other than guard duty) and one company of American infantry fought well, but the day was saved by a Canadian gun battery, the drivers of which checked the enemy advance with their rifles until their guns were able to fire directly at the enemy with shrapnel. The Bolsheviks were eventually repulsed and had to retreat. This was clearly an Allied victory, but they had lost twenty-eight killed and seventy wounded, a loss that could be ill-afforded.

At one stage the Bolsheviks overran the Allied field hospital in the area. The Bolshevik Commander Melochotski entered the hospital and ordered his soldiers to kill all the American and British patients there. The situation was saved, first, by a British medical orderly who produced a good meal and set it before Melochotski together with a big jug of rum. Second, and more important, the Bolshevik Commander's mistress appeared and announced that she would shoot the first soldier who shot an Allied prisoner. Clearly in awe of this formidable lady, the Russian Commander countermanded his order and the British and Americans survived. Melochotski left to continue the Bolshevik attack but was mortally wounded and returned a few hours later to die in his mistress's arms.[29]

During the action, the American company was under the command of a Captain Boyd. At one point when the situation was particularly worrying, it looked as if the American troops were encircled and there was little if any hope of reinforcement because there was no communication with the Allied Headquarters at Archangel. Captain Boyd was cheered by signal lights blinking from a British post on the other side of the River Dvina which, he knew, did have communication with Archangel. Anyone who has had any personal experience of serving in any army of any nationality will recognize only too well what transpired. When the message had been decoded it turned out to be a peremptory demand that he (Captain Boyd) should account immediately for six dozen Red Cross mufflers which had 'been sent to my outfit and not properly receipted for'.[30]

On the railway front, too, the Allies – mainly American with French support, repulsed a Bolshevik attack with commendable steadfastness.

The armistice of 11 November in France and Flanders of course put the whole affair into a totally different light. There could now be no question of the Allies creating another front against the Germans, who had surrendered. J.B. Wilson (later Captain) describes in his diary how he was in the Archangel signal office and watched the operator slowly receiving the news of the armistice from his morse code machine. 'The sensation was terrific but it seemed remote. Our war was still on and we could not get away even if we wanted to' (because of the ice).[31]

Ironside had been having difficulty with the White Russian military commanders. He had succeeded in having the original Commander Durov and his Chief of Staff removed, to be replaced by the much better but flamboyant, although physically small, General Marousheffski. Ironside indeed was somewhat amused but at the same time irritated by the Russian General's habit of personally writing 'long orders of the day' about trivia.[32] Examples of this appear in Appendices A and B (pp 183–5). Furthermore, the Russian officers did not seem to know their soldiers at all. The enormous gulf which had existed between the two in Tsarist times had not been bridged. Many other British officers and soldiers made the same remark.[33]

During the early part of the winter skirmishes continued on the railway front without either side establishing a clear ascendancy. On the Dvina Front, however, the Bolsheviks mounted a second major attack on 19 January 1919. The second largest town in the area was Shenkursk which was some 40 miles up the River Vaga, a tributary of the Dvina which joined that river at Bereznik, where was situated the Allied Headquarters. It was clearly important for the Allies to hold on to Shenkursk, if at all possible, because withdrawal would be extremely bad for the morale, not only of the Allied troops, but also, and more importantly, for the morale of the population of North Russia, some of whom had been enlisted. The establishment and building up of a viable anti-Bolshevik Army was a vital part of the Allied strategy. The Allies had a total of 1,700 troops in the area under the command of the British Colonel Graham, including 400 White Russian conscripts of dubious value. The bulk of the responsibility lay on an American detachment. The Allied forward position was at Ust Padenga, which was about twenty miles south of Shenkursk itself. At 7.30 am the American position came under heavy shellfire and about 1,000 Bolsheviks advanced wearing white smocks which made them difficult to see against the snow. The Americans, under a Captain Odggard, who was badly wounded, fought well and the Bolsheviks were repulsed. The Bolsheviks, however, continued shelling for two days and began to infiltrate around the Allied position both at Ust Padenga and at Shenkursk. The order was given for the evacuation first of Ust Padenga, and on 24 January from Shenkursk itself. Graham (soon to be promoted Brigadier General) organized a withdrawal at night, a most difficult operation, along a track which passed close to a known Bolshevik position. Absolute silence was maintained and the whole Allied force, including a hospital convoy, escaped safely to Bereznik.

The success of this operation, however, could not conceal the fact that the Bolsheviks, who were in fact commanded by an ex-Tsarist general, had won a considerable victory and this had a marked effect on the villages throughout the region who, expecting an eventual Bolshevik final success, became more difficult than ever to enlist in the anti-Bolshevik Army or to help the Allies in other ways. Ironside asked for and received reinforcements of two battalions of British troops from Murmansk one of which, the Yorkshire Regiment, was sent to Onega, the village on the White Sea between the Murmansk railway and Archangel. The battalion had had its trouble on the way to Russia. Private Hirst described in his diary how the battalion had arrived at Dundee on 13 October 1918 and boarded a ship on 15 October:

The soldiers expected to be let off the ship that night but found the gates locked and guarded by military police and men with fixed bayonets. One hundred and fifty men returned to the ship to ask their mates to join them in rushing the gates. The sergeants tried to clear the gangway. The officers are asking the men to play the game but are told, "It's our time now". The colonel draws his revolver and says the next man to get over the side will be shot. He is told that if he does, rifles will be fetched and he will be shot. The Brigadier General who appeared is told what they think of him.[34]

Eventually the ship was towed into midstream and, after a number of breakdowns, sailed to Murmansk, where Hirst found himself acting as a storeman in the Quartermaster's stores, 'better than working outside in the cold . . . every day is just the same and I often lose count of the date and days. The only thing I can reckon on is when Wednesday comes we draw our ration of wood for a week.'

After arriving at Onega, the battalion was ordered to march to Seletskoe on the River Dvina. On 26 February 1919 Ironside received a telegram from Colonel Lavie from the Durham Light Infantry, who had just taken command of the Yorkshire Battalion, to the effect that his battalion had refused to parade. Lavie had the two sergeants who were ringleaders arrested. Later they were court martialled and sentenced to be shot for mutiny (a sentence later commuted to life imprisonment under secret standing orders of King George V) and the battalion marched to Seletskoe without further demur and did well in the subsequent fighting. This insubordination, however, was much exaggerated in the press and elsewhere. A similar, although worse, incident took place in a French battalion which was eventually sent back to France.

There was a further mutiny, this time by the Royal Marines, on the Murmansk Front, much later in September 1919, not long before the final evacuation. The story is told by Lieutenant Roy Smith Hill, Royal Marine Light Infantry, and Lieutenant Colonel Arthur de Winton Kitcat, the latter in a letter to the Colonel Commandant of Royal Marines, Portsmouth.[35]

Smith Hill describes how his battalion of the Royal Marines was expecting to be sent to Schleswig Holstein in August 1919 to supervise the plebiscite, a mainly ceremonial duty, but at the last minute it was diverted to North Russia to bolster the forces available to cover the evacuation.

> We certainly did not expect to fight. In many cases morale was low. The men had not been given the chance to volunteer for Russia (see page 66) The Royal Marines Adjutant General had simply vouched his word for us at the War Office. Colonel Kitcat hadn't helped because he thought it wise not to pay the men the day before we left . . . so that we wouldn't leave any drunks behind. The men had joined up for patriotic reasons; now with the First World War over, in which many of them had fought, they certainly didn't want to lose their lives fighting in Russia. All companies had a number of raw recruits, some very young, and prisoners of war who had recently been returned from Germany and had had no leave.

Smith Hill goes on to describe a failed attack on a village, followed by an unnecessary withdrawal and a chaotic retreat. He describes how ninety-three men were court-martialled and thirteen sentenced to death (not actually carried out). A Captain Watts was cashiered, Smith Hill 'incurred the Lords of the Admiralty's severe displeasure' (not a crippling blow, as he finished his career as a Brigadier) and Lieutenant Colonel Kitcat was placed on the half pay list. With startling, almost abject, modesty, Kitcat's letter to his superior officer reads as follows:

> I have been given such an opportunity as has seldom fallen to the luck of anyone.
>
> Our programme was to take Koikori and burn it. I ought to have succeeded in this without difficulty. I can now see that my best course would have been to have pushed through the wood. I should probably then have effected every object without a casualty. As it was we had four killed and fifteen wounded.
>
> I did not think that I could have made such a hopeless mess of things. I suppose I was suffering from "wind up" but I did not realize it.

One thing stands out perfectly clear is that I am not fit to command troops either in the field or out of it.

I feel I ought to be court martialled and at least cashiered but if I am to be spared that humiliation I must at least retire from the Service I have served so badly.[36]

The British War Cabinet decided on 4 March 1919 that British troops should be withdrawn from North Russia early in the following summer. Churchill, the War Minister, had been pressing for some time for decisive military action against the Bolshevik Government, but it was clear that none of the other members of the War Cabinet, notably Lloyd George, wished to commit themselves to this course of action, nor did the vast bulk of the British people, who were heartily sick of war, care in the least what was happening in Russia and longed for a complete return to peace everywhere. Churchill, however, did get authority to 'make whatever preliminary arrangements he judged necessary to bring about a safe evacuation'. He interpreted this as authorizing the immediate dispatch of two brigades of volunteers re-enlisting for Army service. Churchill wrote, 'It will be made clear to these men that they are only going to extricate their comrades and not for a long occupation of North Russia.'[37]

The word 'volunteer' has a special meaning in the British (and other?) armies. What it hardly ever means is an offer to do something of one's own free will. Private (later Major) B. Pond was a case in point. He said in his diary:

I was called to see Company Sergeant Major Fuller who said to me, "Pond, during your leave a signal was received from brigade asking for volunteers for the North Russian relief force. They especially asked for trained signallers and as the signal was urgent, I sent your name together with mine." I was astounded, having just returned from France, I blurted out, "Sir, I do not want to go to Russia. I had enough of France." He replied, "Perhaps you will not be accepted, we shall have to wait and see." (In the event Pond was posted to a Royal Fusilier battalion.) We were told that a force of British soldiers had been left to look after arms and stores and it was our task to relieve this force . . . we went straight up the Dvina River from Archangel. General Ironside had told

*Brigadier General Sadleir Jackson that his main task was to get
out of Russia without fighting. Some hope! We had 3,000 troops,
the Bolos had 18,000.*[38]

The Second Battalion of the Hampshire Regiment was part of
this relief force. Its regimental history makes it clear that there
was no question of 'volunteers'. It states:

*The troops sent out were originally of low category. It was
decided to relieve these with regulars . . . however, no regular
battalions were as yet sufficiently advanced in reconstruction to
provide much more than a company, and the troops sent out were
really provisional battalions, like that described as the Second
Hampshires who provided a battalion headquarters and one
company, being completed by companies from the Somerset Light
Infantry, the Dorsets and the Wiltshires.*[39]

The Royal Air Force also were heavily, although in comparatively small numbers, involved in the fighting in North
Russia. They had four small airfields, two at or near Archangel,
one at Obozerskaya and one at Bereznik. There were only two
permanent hangars; the rest were under canvas. The extreme
cold made maintenance a great problem. There were no natural
landing places in the forests and swamps and engine failure, a
constant occurrence in the freezing conditions, always led to
a bad crash. Keeping direction in the featureless forests was
extremely difficult. Thirty young pilots, half of them Canadian,
arrived from England: none of them had more than twenty-four
hours' flying experience. There were also some twenty-seven ex-
Tsarist Russian pilots who had far greater experience. All in all,
it was a miracle that the few aircraft provided were able to
achieve anything at all. In fact they were a great help on a
number of occasions, not least in flying Ironside around his far-
flung domain without killing him.

Hudson describes in his journal how his Brigade had a few
aged aeroplanes attached to it. He went over to visit the Brigade
column on the Onega River in a Bristol fighter acting as air
gunner in a seat behind the young pilot. It was his first flight. He
thought he would try out the machine gun with which he had

been equipped and fired it down into a lake. His aeroplane immediately looped the loop – a most alarming experience with no warning. On landing the pilot explained that it was an automatic response to the firing of the machine gun, executed in order to get on the tail of an attacking aircraft.

The morale of the anti-Bolshevik Russians was greatly improved by the arrival of General Miller, like Chaplin a Russian with a surprisingly English name, to take on the post of Governor General of North Russia. He had been an Army Commander in the Tsarist Army, had a good brain and was sensible and sensitive. Ironside and he got on well together, in spite of some political differences over the future of the Baltic States and Finland. Miller applied himself energetically to the task of creating a viable anti-Bolshevik Russian Army and by the end of April had a force of 16,000 men. Their morale depended very heavily upon the success of anti-Bolshevik Russian armies elsewhere, notably in Siberia under Admiral Kolchak and, of course, on the North Russian Front itself. There was a major hiccup on 25 April 1919 when a Russian battalion at Tulgas on the River Dvina mutinied and murdered seven of their officers. Three hundred of their men made off into the forest to join the enemy. Both these elements then attacked the original battalion position. However, remarkably, the remainder of the battalion, who had not mutinied, opened fire and repulsed the attack, although Tulgas had to be evacuated.

Brigadier General Grogan's brigade of the relief force (two battalions of infantry and a battery of mountain howitzers) arrived at Archangel on 27 May. There was much rejoicing among those inhabitants of Archangel who were anti-Bolshevik, and many ceremonial festivities.

The *Hampshire Regiment Journal* of July 1919 includes the following extract from the *Russian North Daily District* newspaper, Archangel of Thursday 29 May 1919:

WELCOME BRITISH VOLUNTEERS. Our hearty, hearty greetings to you! The glad and notable day of your arrival will always remain in our memories as one of the best days of our life – the day when we saw our dear friends and brothers prepared to set out with us and for us to the liberation of our native land, for the re-establishment of our religion, and the rescue of our ruined towns and villages. Hearty greetings to you, noble, generous, brave men who have harkened to the groans and weeping of our women, the cry of our children tormented by hunger, the indescribable sufferings of our fathers and brothers who there, on the other side of the fighting line, are subjected to brutal violence and scorn as well as death by torture.

Warm, sincere Russian thanks to you brother 'soldiers' for your noble effort and for your willingness to help us!

May your coming be blessed and may it strengthen the foundation of our mutual knowledge and of close sympathetic intercourse between our motherland and the great British people.

The *Journal* does not record the reactions of the British soldiers to this very un-British effusion or to the more official welcome by General Miller, the White Russian Governor General (see Appendix C). In any event they were not given much time to savour either of them. The brigade was sent up the Dvina to be followed by Sadleir Jackson's brigade, the other element of the relief force which arrived in Archangel on 5 June.

At that stage it was still hoped that the Allied North Russian force would meet Admiral Kolchak's anti-Bolshevik Russian Army as they advanced to Kotlas. In fact, patrols from Ironside's armies did briefly meet some of Kolchak's force but it was a very temporary affair and, as we shall see elsewhere, Kolchak's armies were comprehensively defeated and had to retreat.

When Ironside received news of Kolchak's defeat, he clearly had to change his plans. He decided to mount a joint British/White Russian attack on the Dvina Front, to shatter the Bolshevik armies in that area, whose morale was already low with hundreds of desertions, to hand over to the Whites and to withdraw all British forces to Archangel for embarkation to Britain, in accordance with his Government's orders.

The Americans had begun to evacuate in early April 1919 on the Dvina Front and a month later on the railway. On this latter front, apparently, the chief worry of the Americans was no longer the Bolshevik armoured train but how to win the baseball championships of North Russia.[40] The 339th Infantry Regiment

69

left Archangel on 14 June. The British showered awards on them but the American General, Richardson, saw this as condescension:

> This has been done apparently in much the same manner as the distribution of gifts by masters to their slaves in the south, in ante bellum days. In other words, it is accompanied throughout by a spirit of superiority on the part of the donors which, although perhaps not intended, nevertheless cannot be concealed. This has become a traditional spirit in the British Army through generations of handling troops of inferior races.[41]

Even their departure from Murmansk on a stopover from Archangel was marred by a fight between American and British soldiers in the port.

Ironside decided to make a small exploratory offensive on the Dvina Front using Russian anti-Bolshevik troops only, but supported by a battalion of Grogan's brigade (the Hampshires). This was to be followed by a major offensive by Sadleir Jackson's brigade. Although the river was now falling, two gunboats were on the scene and could supply supporting fire. The plan was for the Russians to make a frontal attack while the Hampshires, with two mountain howitzers in support, made a wide detour through the forest, arriving at a village named Troitska in the rear of the enemy at the moment of attack. In the event, the Russian attack was a complete success, over 500 prisoners being taken and 100 killed. Most unfortunately the Hampshires took no part in the battle. They completed the detour but their Commanding Officer thought that he was being out-flanked and without engaging the twenty or thirty of the enemy, who were indeed behind him, he withdrew and retired to his starting point. This was, of course, extremely bad from every point of view, not least for the confidence of the anti-Bolshevik units under British command.[42] The Commanding Officer had had a very distinguished career in France. He was not from the Hampshire Regiment, but had been awarded the Victoria Cross while commanding a battalion of another regiment. The failure of the Hampshires was acutely embarrassing, not only for Ironside but also for the Hampshire Regiment itself which had secured for itself a fine record of steadfast courage elsewhere.

The *Hampshire Regimental Journal* of 19 July describes the 'brilliant operation' conducted by the White Russians. It continues, 'The Colonel marched twenty-seven versts (eighteen miles) in tropical heat, but before Troitska was reached the Bolsheviks took *advantage of a temporary indecision* (author's italics), mounted machine guns on a crest and compelled him to retire.' The inference is clear.

In exculpation of his behaviour the Colonel wrote a letter to *The Daily Express* in which he said:

Immediately on arrival at Archangel . . . I was reluctantly but inevitably driven to the following conclusion: that the troops of the relief forces which we were told had been sent out purely for defensive purposes were being used for offensive purposes on a large scale and far into the interior in furtherance of some ambitious plan of campaign, the nature of which we were not allowed to know.

At first he denied being the author, but eventually had to confess. He was court martialled and had to leave the Service.

The Second Battalion of the Hampshire Regiment which, apart from this incident, acquitted itself well during the whole campaign, had to cope with a range of medical problems, as no doubt did other British battalions, due to the climate and the nature of the terrain over which they were operating. They had few casualties due to enemy action but the *Regimental History* of the Hampshire Regiment sets out their medical record in Russia for two months as follows:

		Officers	Other Ranks
July	To Hospital	6	46
	From Hospital	2	21
	To Base Hospital	10	
August	To Hospital	2	43
	From Hospital	3	25
	To Base Hospital		3

Ironside now had to cope with two further mutinies. On 7 July a company of the Slavo/British Legion known as Dyer's Battalion, named after its original Commanding Officer, mutinied and killed five British and four Russian officers. A hundred men deserted to the Bolsheviks, the unit was disarmed and turned into a labour battalion. This was particularly worrying for Ironside who had put a lot of faith in this, largely British, creation.

On 19 July there occurred the mutiny at Onega and on the railway front which was described by Charles Hudson in Chapter One. A Captain J.B. Wilson was in Onega as one of the British officers with the anti-Bolshevik Russian battalion which mutinied. He was nearly shot, but was then tethered between two mounted horses and had to run for many miles before halting and being interrogated by a commissar who tried, unsuccessfully, to convert him to Communism. He was then sent to Archangel on parole to try to arrange an exchange of prisoners, which was unsuccessful. He returned to captivity and was incarcerated in Moscow. At first this was not a bad experience as he was allowed out again on parole. He received food parcels from the Danish Red Cross. He and his fellow prisoners were visited by the high-ranking Bolshevik Litvinov, who tried to arrange mail for them. He was eventually exchanged for some Bolshevik prisoners in Brixton jail.[43] George Roupell was not so lucky. He was Staff Captain to the Turner brigade (with Charles Hudson as Brigade Major) in Obozerskaya and was sent to visit the anti-Bolshevik battalion at Onega. He, too, was captured there after the mutiny. He was nearly shot and then made to march – not run – 115 miles in ten days. He finished up in prison in Moscow and was not finally released until May 1922.[44]

Throughout the intervention in North Russia the Bolshevik propaganda machine had been working hard to convince the Allied soldiers that the real objective of their masters was to crush the Revolution in Russia, to reinstate the old regime there and to prevent the spreading of revolution into the capitalist West. They should, therefore, refuse to fight against their Russian fellow workers, the Bolsheviks. An example of a leaflet distributed to the Americans and British is attached at

Appendix D. This had very little, if any, effect and was on the level with broadcasts by Joyce (Lord Haw-Haw) to Britain in the Second World War, listened to by the author as a boy with great delight. Quite unconnected with this, however, there were many British 'volunteers' and others who, at some stage, were approaching mutiny. In his diary A.E. Thompson, a wireless trained Royal Engineer, describes his and other feelings in the following terms:

11 November 1918 – The armistice caused a flutter here and much regret that we are unaffected, for everyone is fed up.

10 February 1919 – The men out here are all 'category' and it is simply scandalous that they should have to be fighting now and under such conditions when there is peace on all other fronts. We are muzzled and cannot get the truth out of the country. We see cuttings from English papers saying everybody is contented and that we are getting special food etc. All rot! ...up the line they cannot even get bread and have to munch biscuits as hard as any brick. And still we smile doggedly.

18 February – Put in charge of WT station. Made Corporal on 26 February. Went to lecture at YMCA about aims of Allies. Strong opinions. I made a speech [clearly subversionary!] *loudly applauded.*

March 18 – We are having a very bad time on the various fronts, being hopelessly outnumbered. How the boys stick it in this climate beats me and mostly B1 and B2 (categories) at that. Everybody is fed up with the whole show and there is much unrest. Incidents approaching mutiny. Three men were to be shot for inciting the troops to mutiny. Two reprieved.

25 March – Getting very exciting. Much talk of another mutiny, in town. All the peasant class in the town are Bolshevik. Thirty cases of frostbite.

6 June – Overwhelmed with traffic from Omsk. Generals Miller and Kolchak send each other telegrams of terrific length. Excited about volunteers (sic) coming out to relieve us. Out of mire. Expected Oberskaya to fall. If it had it could have been all up with us at Archangel.

18 June – Russian General conferred on me the Russian Silver Medal for devotion to duty. Also the Order of St Anne. Great party.

26 June – Went before CO for writing a letter expressing my thoughts on our compulsory situation in the country. It was returned to me with threats of disciplinary action.

1 July – Promoted Sergeant.

11 July – Relief party thought they were going to walk through the Bolos. The first day the Hants went over the top. They lost fifty men and refused to carry on. Their Colonel has been sent home. Villages we held all the winter with a handful of men had been lost and Pinega is surrounded. Some start!!! Our monitors are cut off and are being pounded with heavy artillery. General wind up.

15 July – Heard that Dyer's battalion (Slavo/British legion) have murdered their English officers. Free fight between Russians and Britons in Archangel tonight. Five hundred in melee.

18 July – Half of Dyer's battalion taken to Bakharitza to be shot.

25 July – Onega captured today by Bolos. We are in a fairly desperate situation here. I have only eight men on the station and a guard of four men. Only fifty rounds each. I don't get a wink of sleep and feel absolutely done up.[45]

There are a number of inaccuracies in this diary, as is probably to be expected. Thompson was clearly what was known as a 'barrack room lawyer', accentuating the negative and ignoring the positive and he was by no means typical of the British Army in North Russia. However, his diary does show the problems with which Ironside and his fellow commanders were faced. There was undoubtedly a strong feeling of unease about the aims of the enterprise and the fact that soldiers were being asked to fight again so soon after the massive and shattering experience of the First World War. However, this never really surfaced and the bulk of the British Army in North Russia remained steadfast and loyal as is clearly shown in the vast majority of their diaries. There was only one minor incident of disaffection among the British Army (page 64) and that was soon dealt with. It did not spread. The marine mutiny was successfully hushed up.

As always on active service, life was full of contrasts, some of them being almost incredibly stark as is shown in Major Gawthorpe's diaries. Much of his time was spent fishing, shooting and entertaining or being entertained by Russians in the villages:

> *20 July – Went into a village, played rounders with children. Church parade. Court martial on Davis. Sixty days Field Punishment. Got off lightly.*
> *29 July – Singsong with host's daughter.*
> *30 July – Entertained Russian General, wives, staff.*
> *31 July – Arranged to get ex-Dyer prisoner sent back to be shot. Had a singsong in Mess.*
> *2 August – Met my host and wife, most excellent type of Russian tradesman. Priest arrived and walked up to Ivan and said a prayer for the harvest, the house and the occupants. Then shook hands all round, had a couple of quick brandies and went on to the next house (sixty-eight houses in village).*
> *7 August – Drove off to the sports in a four in hand with Rotes and Foster as postilions.*
> *16 August – Went fishing and duck shooting.*
> *20 August – Fishing, started draughts tournament.*
> *5 September – Fairly suddenly told to be prepared to depart for England.*
> *21 September – Went down Dvina.*
> *25 September – Loaded small arms and ammunition to be dumped at sea.*
> *7 October – Left via White Sea to Lerwick.*[46]

General Rawlinson, who had commanded an Army in France and was extremely popular with all ranks, was sent out to command all troops in North Russia in order to coordinate their evacuation. He arrived at Archangel on 11 August 1919, bringing with him four Mark V and two Whippet tanks to help cover the final withdrawal. The final attack by Sadleir Jackson's brigade and the bulk of the White Russian Army in the north had started the day before. As Ironside put it, 'It was a triumphant success.'[47]

This bald statement as to the outcome of this, or indeed any other, military operation begs a whole lot of questions and conceals a great deal of anguish, courage, fear, heroism or, perhaps, cowardice. Bit part actors in the drama might well not recognize the action as they saw it from the post facto descriptions of it. The outcome of any military operation depends, of course, not only on the leadership, or lack of it, of those in command but, probably more importantly, on the instant decisions taken by hundreds, or perhaps thousands, of individuals. One such was Private (later Major) D. Pond of the Staffordshire Regiment, who had been posted to the Royal Fusiliers. He captured some of the excitement and agony of the action in his diary. He was in charge of A Company's signals in the attack on Gorodok on the Dvina Front:

My section was very heavily loaded, myself and six other signallers. We carried reels of D111 cable, lucas lamps and helios, trench wireless sets (not operational in close country), full equipment, rifle, extra bandoliers, two grenades etc.

9 August 1919 – Very warm, mosquitoes. Some youngsters started to lag, had to curse them to keep up. I was twenty years old. [This was clearly inserted later.] *Job was to pass round the flanks of the enemy without arousing suspicion. Wade through fast flowing river. Hold rifles, Lewis gun over heads, got there 1.30 am. Dark, cold, wet, miserable. Rum up at 2.30 am, but only lime juice. During night gas attack on Bolo position (see page 77). Just before dawn continued advance around flanks. Front attack no progress. Artillery fire given by* HMS Humber. *Pinned down by small arms fire. Told by company commander to get HQ to shell first objective. We are held up. Did so. Then were shelled by our people. Told to tell them to stop but line cut. Told to go back and mend line. Went back mended one break. Then hit in foot. Applied first field dressing. Got hold of pony, mended six breaks. Got through to battalion. Got shelling in right place. Captured Gorodok. Second in command killed. Told to be evacuated – but carried on. Went to church to establish lucas signalling lamp. Sixty Bolos rushed. Then they surrendered. Evacuated by Droshky. Went to hospital ship in Troitska. Got back to England. Issued with Russian Cross of St George for gallantry. Still unpaid Lance Corporal.*[48]

The White Russians attacked on the railway front on 29 August. The attack went well and nearly 1,000 prisoners were taken. The Royal Air Force was a great help here, dropping 361 gas bombs.[49] Further help was supplied by an Australian company which broke the line in front of them by a bayonet charge.[50]

The successful attacks on both fronts fully achieved their objectives – disrupting the Bolshevik forces while the British evacuated North Russia – and the evacuation of the British Army went off without a hitch. The ships also took with them 911 White Russian military men and 4,685 Russian civilians, plus a few from Murmansk.[51] They also, on orders from the War Office, took with them 101 Bolshevik hostages for exchange with British prisoners held by the Bolsheviks. Many of the British soldiers involved had hoped for some recognition in the form of a special medal commemorating service in North Russia. But this was refused – an absurd politically motivated decision. The last British soldiers left Archangel on 27 September 1919 and on 12 October from Murmansk.

Commander J. Bower, who was in HMS *Moth* covering the final British evacuation from Archangel, summed up in his diary what, no doubt, many British servicemen must have thought:

> It is certainly an unsatisfactory business trying to help people who may – and do – turn against us at any moment. There is practically nothing to choose between the Bolo soldiers we capture and the Russian volunteer battalions in training round here; it was merely chance in which part of the country they found themselves when the obligation of taking up arms came along . . . One hardly blames many of the local brand of "friendly Russians" in a way since they know on the departure of the British – becoming an open secret now – the Bolos will murder all – of whatever sex or age – whom they know or suspect to have had friendly relations with us. It is certainly politic to hedge a little.[52]

When writing or reading an account of this nature it is too easy to forget the atmosphere in which the various operations were conducted. Any civil war arouses feelings of intense hatred and Russia was no exception. There were many incidents of appalling savagery on both sides which in their turn, of course, led to a vicious circle of murderous revenge (see also pp 137, 160).

In his journal Charles Hudson describes how a very beautiful young Russian nurse, a Baltic Baroness, had asked for an interview with him after the mutiny at Onega, described in Chapter One. She was engaged to the British Brigade Intelligence Officer. She said that she had a matter of urgent importance to discuss with Hudson. Thinking that she was about to disclose some impending mutiny, he agreed. There had been a number of courts martial of the Russian mutineers and several had been condemned to death. She said that the Russian Commanding Officer had refused her permission to witness the executions and she wanted the British General to overrule him.

Nothing I could say shook her determination. She became almost hysterical and stormed at us. Ever since she had seen her own father shot she had sworn to be present at the shooting of some Bolsheviks. She could never be at peace until she had. What business, she said, had anyone to deny her this? As she raved on, I saw, through the window behind her, a party of dejected-looking prisoners, surrounded by armed guards, being marched down the platform, and I realized that if I could keep her talking a little longer she would be too late . . . In the hope of pacifying her I told her the General was out but I would see what I could do to persuade the OC hospital to release her, although I could make no promises. Then I sat down and wasted time in writing a note to her Commanding Officer. In it I said, if he could detain her a little longer, the executions would be over.

I was told later that as soon as he had released her, she had run nearly a mile round by a circuitous route, to avoid the guards surrounding the place of execution, and though too late to see the shooting, she had insisted on being shown the horribly mutilated bodies before they were buried. To me it seemed almost impossible to believe that this educated, and in every other way apparently well balanced and refined girl, could have been capable of this. I had yet a lot to learn.

Seaman Tom Spurgeon was in Murmansk with the marines in March 1918:

While I was there I met a Russian Officer who could speak better English than I could. I suppose he was about thirty and he had been a solicitor in Moscow before the Revolution. One day he asked me if I could get ashore the following morning. I managed

78

this and met him. We walked together, talking away as we always did about the Western way of life. Without noticing too much we strolled into a park where there were a number of soldiers and dissidents, including women and children. When the soldiers saw us approach the civilians were all lined up. Then, as calm as anything, this Officer I had been talking to walked down the line and shot every one of them through the back. He then went back down the line and if any were breathing he shot them through the head. To him it was like having breakfast. There were women and small children but it didn't seem to worry him at all. I remember clearly some of the bodies quivering on the ground. I can never forget it. I am haunted by it even now.

One of the major lessons of the campaign was summed up by General Sir Henry Wilson, the Chief of the Imperial General Staff, in his report on the Archangel campaign. 'The lesson to stand out above all others was that once a military force is involved in operations on land it is almost impossible to limit the magnitude of its operations. One hundred and fifty British Marines landed at Murmansk in April 1918. A year later more than 18,000 British troops were involved.' Two hundred and twenty-two American and 317 British soldiers lost their lives.

It took a little longer than some expected for the Bolsheviks to defeat the anti-Bolsheviks in North Russia, mainly because they were devoting their attention to the south. But on 21 February 1920 the 154th Red Infantry Regiment marched into Archangel, the inhabitants of which received the conquerors with as much enthusiasm as they had received the Allies eighteen months earlier. Just before this, on 19 February, General Miller fled by icebreaker to Norway and thence to Paris, where, in September 1937, he was to be kidnapped by Bolshevik agents and almost certainly murdered.

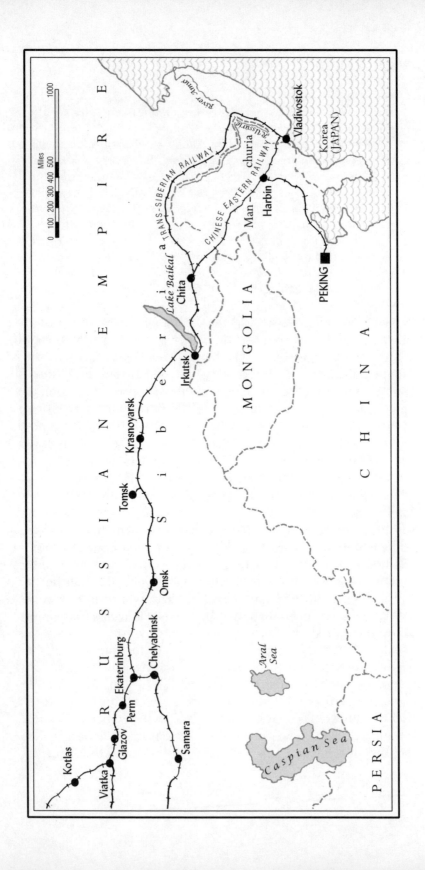

Chapter Four

THE FAR EAST

In October 1918 Sergeant Jupe of the 1st/9th Cyclist Battalion of the Hampshire Regiment, a territorial formation, found himself in India doing nothing very much. The battalion had hoped to be involved in the war in France but to their disappointment had been sent to India. On the 18th of that month orders were received by their Commanding Officer to go to Siberia. Sergeant Jupe recorded that the Regiment, 'was to proceed to Vladivostok, make its way across Siberia, turn the German Army out of the country, put a stop to the Bolshevik Revolution, and then await further orders'.[1] Unsurprisingly, in the event matters were not quite so simple.

During the war the Russians had organized a detachment of Czech and Slovak troops who were living in Russia in order to use them in the struggle against Germany. These people were willing recruits and were encouraged by the Czech National Council which was established in Paris and which was hoping to gain recognition of Czecho-Slovak national status from the Allies. They fought well. After the fall of the Tsar this small force was greatly augmented by the addition of Czech and Slovak prisoners of war. Eventually a whole army corps was established. When the Russian Army collapsed, the question of the destiny of the Czech corps became a burning issue. The Czech Council wished to transfer the whole corps of some 42,000 men to the Western Front and the French, desperate for manpower, became almost obsessive about the idea. In December 1917 they recognized the Czech Army as autonomous and placed it under the direction of the French Supreme Command. However, the

Czechs clearly could not reach the Western Front by travelling west since the Germans were in total control of the whole of that area. An alternative was to travel right across Siberia and embark at Vladivostok. Trotsky, as Soviet Foreign Minister, accepted this and they began the journey with Soviet acquiescence – with the proviso that the Czechs should surrender nearly all their arms. At this stage the British conceived the idea that half the Czech corps should move north to Archangel, ostensibly in order to return to the Western Front via that port, but in fact to support the Allied force in North Russia. This plan, which never really got off the ground, became the basis of the instructions given to General Ironside in command of the Allied forces at Archangel.

The Czechs began this movement along the railway towards Vladivostok. Initially seventy trains were used for this operation, but later this number was considerably increased. There were a number of hiccups of one sort or another until a major incident occurred at Chelyabinsk. The March 1918 German/Russian Peace Treaty of Brest-Litovsk provided for the return to their home countries of all the 800,000 or so German and Austro/Hungarian prisoners of war of whom a number, mostly Austrian and Hungarian in origin, were in Siberia. It happened on 14 May 1918 that an eastbound train full of Czech and Slovak soldiers found itself stationary opposite a westbound train full of Hungarian returning prisoners of war. There was no love lost between the two. The Czechs saw the Hungarians as their erstwhile oppressors, while the Hungarians saw the Czechs as traitors. A Hungarian threw a missile at a Czech. The Czechs lynched him and the eventual upshot was that Trotsky gave orders that any Czech found with a weapon was to be shot on the spot. The Czechs decided to fight their way through to Vladivostok. Between May and August 1918 they took control of virtually the whole of the Trans-Siberian Railway from Samara as far as Vladivostok, where at first the Bolsheviks managed to retain control of the town and port. The Czechs entered Ekaterinburg just too late to avert the assassination of the Tsar and his entire family on 16 July 1918.

Meanwhile, if anything, even more extraordinary events were

taking shape. The Japanese had declared war on Germany in late August 1914 but had made virtually no contribution to the struggle. Their ostensible reason for the declaration of war was fear of a successful Germany becoming a dominant power in the Far East. But they also had greedy eyes on parts of Siberia and Manchuria. In these circumstances the French and British military staff had the extraordinary idea that a Japanese Army could be transported across the Trans-Siberian railway from Vladivostok to start up a new front against Germany in the Carpathians. The distance involved was 7,000 miles and the railway system could not possibly cope with the necessary tonnage. Furthermore, the Soviet authorities would clearly be bitterly opposed to what would come down to a massive Japanese invasion of their territory and, in any event, the Japanese never had the slightest intention of doing anything of the sort.

However, Japan did have a great interest in a far more limited intervention. Apart from her designs on various Far Eastern provinces, Manchuria and China, she wished to safeguard the great naval base at Vladivostok against any occupation from a hostile power and, with their ideas of world revolution, the Soviets probably would be hostile.

The Americans, too, had a great interest in developments in the Far East. They certainly did not wish to be involved themselves, but neither did they wish to allow Japan complete hegemony over the whole region. Furthermore, a number of bands of freebooting soldiers of various political and ethnic origins were ranging around the area, looking for booty. The swashbuckling, sinister and enormously cruel Cossack leader Semenov had established himself astride the Chinese Eastern Railway where he managed to raise a considerable army, terrifying the local population and antagonizing Bolshevik and anti-Bolshevik elements alike. In Manchuria, nominally part of China, the Tsarist Russian Dimitri Horvat, the General Manager of the Chinese Eastern Railway was the most powerful figure. A provisional 'Government of Autonomous Siberia' had been set up by the Social Revolutionary (anti-Bolshevik) party, headed by a native of Odessa, Peter Derber. In addition to these elements there were the Chinese, the British, French and

Japanese diplomatic representatives, together with the old Tsarist functionaries who were inescapably involved. It was a mess. The situation was bordering on complete chaos. On top of this the Allies had stockpiled vast (about 648,000 tons) quantities of military stores in Vladivostok with the idea that it should be sent across the Trans-Siberian Railway to the Russian armies in the West. There was the fear that these stores might be transferred across Russia to help the German armies.

The first Allied intervention in the Far East was in fact undertaken by the British, who sent a cruiser, the *Suffolk*, from Hong Kong to Vladivostok to keep an eye on these stores. The Japanese, not to be outdone, immediately sent two more warships there. The Americans followed suit with another cruiser.

The British intervention was a highly symbolic gesture, certainly in one quarter. Florence Farmborough, an English governess in Moscow in 1914 who had joined the Russian Red Cross, had survived the war in the West and had, with a number of beleaguered colleagues, travelled on the Trans-Siberian Railway across Russia in an attempt to escape the Bolshevik chaos, described in her book, her feelings on arriving at Vladivostok.

> *In that harbour four large cruisers were anchored and one of them was flying the Union Jack. Oh! The relief! The comfort! The security! Who will ever know all that this glorious flag symbolled for us travel-weary refugees? It was as though we had heard a dear familiar voice bidding us "welcome home". As I write these words I can feel my heart palpitating with emotion; it holds a depth of gratitude that can never be expressed. That one glimpse of the Union Jack dispelled all our fears, quietened all our doubts, answered all our questions. It was a truly wonderful homecoming and one which we had least expected. The Union Jack was our talisman, our guarantee, our surety!*

As was the case in North Russia, after considerable pressure, both internal and from the British and French Governments, the Americans were also persuaded to change their mind about intervention in the Far East. The decisive argument with

1. Lenin in about 1919.
(Illustrated London News)

THE DOVE AT SEA
Bird of Peace: "Excuse me, but is this the ark?"
Man of War: "Dunno nothin' about no ark; but we're for ark-angel, if that's any use to you."

3. Trotsky reviewing Red Army troops in Moscow, 1919.   *(Illustrated London News)*

4. General Ironside
   with small friend
   near Archangel.

5. British seaplane
   attacking
   Bolshevik train in
   North Russia.
   (Illustrated London
   News)

6. Russian recruiting march through Archangel. *(Illustrated London News)*

7. A British soldier in Arctic kit at Archangel. *(Illustrated London News)*

8. The first British troops disembark at Vladivostok. *(Illustrated London News)*

9. British warships in floating ice in the Baltic.   *(Illustrated London News)*

10. General Yudenich.
    (Illustrated London News)

11. British officers on the Trans-Siberian
    Railway.   *(Illustrated London News)*

12. Allied warships at Murmansk. *(Illustrated London News)*

13. Allied warships at Vladivostok. *(Illustrated London News)*

14. Czech, British and Japanese sailors parade in Vladisvostok.

(Illustrated London News)

15. Men of the Royal Navy guarding destroyed trains in North Russia.

(Illustrated London News)

16. General Denikin *(centre)* with his staff behind him. *(Illustrated London News)*

17. Cossacks with dismounted Russian infantry. *(Illustrated London News)*

18. Bolshevik ships in Kronstadt Harbour before the British attack.

(Illustrated London News)

19. German gunners prepare to bombard Riga. *(Illustrated London News)*

President Wilson was that the Czechs were in urgent need of support in Siberia. President Wilson agreed to only a small-scale intervention of 7,000 men by the Americans and Japanese alike who were only to be used to help the Czechs against German and Austrian prisoners of war, to guard Vladivostok and not to interfere in the internal affairs of Russia. Of course, in practice, there was no question of the appearance of any outside body without the Bolsheviks being convinced that it was interference in their internal affairs.

On 17 July President Wilson sent the Allied Governments a memorandum, 'It was the clear and fixed judgement of the Government of the United States that military intervention . . . would add to the present sad confusion in Russia rather than cure it, injure her rather than help her.' The United States could not 'take part in such intervention or sanction it in principle'. The United States Government felt that military action in Russia was admissible 'only to help the Czechoslovaks consolidate their forces and get into successful cooperation with their Slavic kinsmen and to steady any efforts at self-government or self-defence in which the Russians themselves may be willing to accept assistance. Whether from Vladivostok or from Murmansk and Archangel, the only legitimate object for which American or Allied troops can be employed . . . is to guard military stores which may subsequently be needed by Russian forces and to render such aid as may be acceptable to the Russians in the organization of their own self-defence.' The memorandum went on to say that it only applied to American forces and they did not wish to limit the choices of policy of their allies.

The American Government hoped 'to carry out the plans for safe-guarding the rear of the Czechoslovaks operating from Vladivostok in a way that would place it and keep it in close cooperation with a small military force like its own from Japan, and if necessary from the other Allies.' The document then went on with almost unbelievable naivety to say that the United States Government hoped 'to take advantage of the earliest opportunity to send to Siberia a commission of merchants, agricultural experts, labour advisers, Red Cross representatives and agents of the Young Men's Christian Association accustomed to organizing the best methods of spreading useful information and rendering educational help of a modest sort, in some systematic manner to relieve the immediate economic necessities of the people.' This at a time when, the chaos in Siberia was total.

Thus, the other Allies, including the Japanese, were able to intervene almost at will. Within a month there were over 70,000 Japanese troops in Siberia and Manchuria. In fact the Americans themselves, although they sent troops to Siberia, never really became involved there since, unlike in the north, the American troops remained under American command and they had a resolute Commander who refused to be deflected from the orders he had been given by his Government. But the President, by his ambiguous and vacuous memorandum, in effect gave *carte blanche* to the other Allies, and notably to the Japanese, to take action as they saw fit.

In practice the Japanese advanced into Eastern Siberia and Manchuria, treating the local inhabitants with scant respect for any rights they may have thought they had. The British and the French appointed High Commissioners to Siberia, and the Japanese, whose General was nominally commanding all the Allied troops in the area, established a Department of Political Affairs, since the Army would be in charge of political as well as military affairs. General Knox, who had a great knowledge of Russian affairs having been military attaché in Petrograd since 1914, was sent to Siberia as head of the British Staff at the Japanese military headquarters.

The British and Japanese forces began to disembark at Vladivostok on 3 August and the Americans began to land their 7,000 men on 16 August, the American General Graves arriving on the same day. His instructions were, 'To safeguard the rear of the Czechoslovakian operations from Vladivostok and to guard military stores which may subsequently be needed by Russian forces.' It was not clear which Russian forces were involved! Graves had been briefed by the Secretary for War for ten minutes in a room at Kansas City railway station and given an aide memoire. The briefing ended, 'Watch your step; you'll be walking on eggs loaded with dynamite. God bless you and goodbye.'

At that time the aims of three main protagonists, therefore, were as follows:

The British hoped to help the Czechs in thwarting German plans (which did not exist) to dominate Russia and to support any anti-Bolshevik Russian elements which might succeed in their struggle against the Bolshevik regime.

The Japanese were clearly intent on seizing as much of Manchuria as they could.

The American aim, which was to safeguard the Czech rear as they moved to the east to join up with their compatriots in Europe, had already been achieved before they arrived.

The British contingent, the first on the scene, consisted of the 25th Battalion of the Middlesex Regiment commanded by Lieutenant Colonel John Ward, Labour Member of Parliament for Stoke-on-Trent and a pioneer of the Trade Union Movement. The battalion was in Hong Kong at the time and was composed of men graded B1 (unfit for active service in a theatre of war). It came to be known among other British soldiers in Siberia as the 'Hernia Battalion'. 'Poor old men, they ought never to have been sent here.'[3] Colonel Ward, who subsequently wrote a book, *With the Diehards* [nickname for the Middlesex Regiment] *in Siberia*, must have been a remarkable character. Victor Cazalet, the ADC to General Knox, head of the British Military Mission, referred to him as a 'gasbag'[4], but he must have had far more character than is implied by that term. He held his battalion together, apparently composed of old, unfit men, through an appallingly difficult period of total confusion and near chaos against a background of extreme cold.

An earlier incident gave a flavour of him. On the way to Hong Kong on 6 February 1917 the ship they were travelling in hit a mine off South Africa and began to sink. The 'fall in' was sounded and Ward addressed his men:

Officers and men of the 25th. You have now the supreme test of your lives, the one moment we all ought to have lived for. Remember that you are Englishmen. All the best traditions of our country and race are in your keeping. You are a member of one of the most famous regiments in the British Army. Pray God that you do not sully its honour. Obey orders and we may be able to save you all; but if we cannot then let us finish like English gentlemen.[5]

In the event the ship did not sink.

At the beginning of the twenty-first century it is difficult to imagine circumstances when this kind of appeal could possibly be acceptable. But it clearly struck a chord. The phrase 'politically incorrect' had not yet entered the consciousness of Britain.

In fact Ward[6] stated that he had originally been warned in November 1917 that he and his battalion might be sent to a 'very cold climate', but this was cancelled in January 1918. Ward goes on to say that his battalion's job was 'to assist the orderly elements of Russian Society to organize themselves under a national government and to resurrect and reconstruct the Russian Front'. He went on, 'Under German directions the Soviets had released their German and Austrian prisoners of war (of which there were many thousands), armed and organized them into formidable armies and set them to the work of terrorizing the Russian people and destroying the country.' It is difficult to imagine a more vague and misleading instruction. Who were these orderly elements? And of course there were very few, if any, German and Austrian prisoners of war fighting in any army in the East.

When the Middlesex Battalion landed they were greeted by a Czech band which struck up the National Anthem while a petty officer from HMS *Suffolk* unfolded the Union Jack. To applause by a 'tremendous crowd of people we marched through the town to a saluting base where parties of Czech, Cossack, Russian troops and Japanese, American and Russian sailors were drawn up, all of whom (except the Japanese) came to the present as we passed.'

Ward was told that the Czech and Cossack troops on the River Ussurie Front to the north were under considerable pressure from Bolshevik troops commanded by German and Austrian officers and he was asked for help. The War Office agreed by cable that half the battalion should be used for this purpose. Ward found himself in command of a mixed bag of 400 British riflemen with a machine-gun section of four Maxims, a company of Czech infantry (about 200 men) and 400 Cossack cavalry. After a very disagreeable fortnight with his soldiers without tents or mosquito nets (vital in an area infected by large numbers of these bloodsucking insects) Ward was told that he had to hand over command to the French Major Pichon who was arriving with a French contingent. After an action between a Bolshevik and a British armoured train the latter with naval twelve pounders manned by sailors from HMS *Suffolk*, the Allied position was outflanked and became extremely precarious. However, a battalion of Japanese troops, together with a battery of Japanese guns, appeared on the scene, followed by a whole Japanese division, whereupon Ward was told that he and his troops were to come under the command of the Japanese Colonel Inagaki. The overall command was to be held by the Japanese General Oie. This was confirmed in a message from the War Office on 18 August.

During the ensuing battle Ward found himself commanding a reserve consisting of 200 Middlesex Regiment, one company of French infantry, one company of Japanese infantry and 600 Cossack cavalry, a mixed bag to say the least. In fact, in the chaos, Ward led an Allied attack in conjunction with an armoured train. He gives a vivid description of a very diffuse and chaotic action in which the Japanese suffered over 600 casualties. However, 'not a man of the 25th was hit. We had many cases of prostration but, in view of the category of my unit, not more than was to be expected, considering the strenuous month's work they'd undergone. One and all behaved like Englishmen – the highest eulogy that can be passed on the conduct of men.'[7]

Private Reardon[8] noted that, having arrived at the front line he dug trenches for three days. They were then joined by French troops and were heavily shelled. The first division of Japanese troops arrived on 22 August. The Middlesex advanced with the Japanese, with the Czechs and French in support. 'The Japs made a brilliant victory.'

Not surprisingly, there were different versions of this comparatively small action but, be that as it may, the Bolsheviks were comprehensively defeated and Ward was ordered to take his battalion to Omsk on garrison duty to help preserve order in the town. On the way there by the Chinese Eastern Railway they were held up by the Japanese. They were eventually allowed to proceed, but this incident, and a later occurrence when General Knox himself was similarly treated, demonstrate the very mixed relations within the Allied alliance. The Japanese regarded eastern Siberia and Manchuria as their own bailiwick. According to Ward, and others, they behaved with total arbitrary cruelty and confirmed the worst fears of the Russians, Bolshevik and anti-Bolshevik alike, whose hatred of them was confirmed and emphasized. Having left Vladivostok on 24 September the Middlesex Regiment arrived at Omsk on 26 October.

When temporarily impeded by the Japanese, General Knox was on his way to Omsk where he hoped to be able to organize a coherent anti-Bolshevik Front from the many disparate elements ranging from anarchists to left-wing social revolutionaries to freebooting bandits who were competing for power. Having originally supported Ataman Semenov who, it was hoped, would supplant the Bolsheviks in Siberia, the British had realized their error and had changed their policy from support to opposition. The Japanese, however, saw Semenov as a useful tool and were giving him help with arms, money and some officer staff. A Foreign Office memorandum dealt with the Japanese in no uncertain terms:

> The Japanese accompanied their entry into Siberia with the usual proclamation of disinterestedness. The proclamation affirmed the constant desire of Japan to promote relations of enduring friendship with Russia and the Russian people and reaffirmed her avowed policy of respecting the territorial integrity of Russia and of abstaining from all interference in her internal politics. Nevertheless, a self-seeking and obstructive attitude on the part of the Japanese became evident at once ... Their progress through the country was marked by utter contempt of the population and they proceeded to occupy pacified territory in the rear with a force five times stronger than was required whilst doing nothing to help the half-armed, half-clothed Russians and Czechs to fight. The immediate impression it created was that they were endeavouring

by every means in their power to prevent the establishment of a strong central government with a single army and their behaviour was generally described as that of a people who intend to annex what they have occupied.[9]

As for Semenov, the Japanese protégé, he was described by a witness as 'presiding over . . . an atmosphere of laziness, rodomontade, alcohol, lucrative requisitions, dirty money and the killing of the innocent'.[10]

It was into this chaotic scene that the British inserted the remarkable figure of Admiral Kolchak. Having distinguished himself as a young man in arctic exploration and then in the Russo/Japanese war, service in the Baltic and Black Seas culminated in command of the Russian Black Sea fleet at the unprecedentedly early age of forty-four. He was horrified by the Russian peace with Germany at Brest-Litovsk, seeing continuation of the war as a matter of honour. He offered his services to the British Government in any capacity, if necessary as a private soldier on the Western Front. He was clearly a considerable figure of value to the Allies and, after a series of moves from the United States to Tokyo, to Shanghai, to Commander-in-Chief of the Russian forces in the Chinese Railway Zone, he appeared in Omsk. Honest, almost to a fault, he was a solitary dour figure but with a powerful personality which impressed all who met him – in particular General Knox who was, throughout, a great supporter.

Affairs at Omsk went from bad to worse. The nominal government, a five-man directorate, lost control of the situation. Every night as soon as darkness set in rifle and revolver shots and shouts could be heard in all directions.[11] The outcome of this chaos was a coup whereby four of the directorate were arrested and Admiral Kolchak, who had in fact been appointed Minister for War at the time, was installed as Supreme Governor. Ward realized that a coup was in progress and alerted his battalion, installing machine guns covering the main streets in the town. He was also able to prevent the probable execution of the four ministers of the directorate and to arrange for their safe conduct to China with a guard of British soldiers. Kolchak was initially successful in bringing coherence to the various anti-Bolshevik sections and in creating a unified army which had a number of successes, eventually advancing as far as Perm and Glasoff, only 300 miles east of Petrograd and sixty miles south of Kotlas. However, the Czechs, who, for a variety of reasons, hated and distrusted Kolchak, refused to take any part in support of his Army.

There were suspicions that the coup had been organized by the British and in particular by Knox and Ward. The French General Janine, who had just arrived at Vladivostok to head the French Military Mission and to take personal command of all the Czech troops in Siberia, actually wrote a report to the French Ministry of War in which he said that the British had organized the coup so that they could have a 'Government to themselves' in Siberia.[12] There was no truth in this accusation, but it again demonstrated the extreme difficulty of joint military/political activities without a single coherent plan.

In fact, apart from eight naval guns manned by marines which were in action for a short time in European Russia 6,105 miles from Vladivostok, and Colonel Ward's short foray described on page 89, the British active military contribution to the anti-Bolshevik force in Siberia was confined to the supply of arms, including a complete set of equipment for 100,000 men, and to the training of 3,000 anti-Bolshevik Russian troops under the auspices of General Knox, who had a large Military Mission based at Omsk. He also set up a training school for Russian officers and NCOs with a number of British instructors on an island in the bay of Vladivostok. On 15 February 1919 the first class of 1,000 officers and NCOs graduated.

The second British unit, the 1st/9th Cyclist Battalion of the Hampshire Regiment arrived in Vladivostok (without their bicycles) on 28 November 1918. The temperature in India had been 116 degrees in the shade. In Siberia they were to encounter temperatures of 58 degrees below zero. On arrival, unlike the Middlesex Regiment, however, they were issued with very good Canadian arctic clothing. Their orders were to relieve the Middlesex Regiment at Omsk. They set off by the Chinese Eastern Railway on 18 December. On 25 December they reached Chita, where they marched through the town and paid respects to the notorious Ataman Semenov, who appeared to be in control of the area. They arrived at Omsk on 7 January 1919.[13] There they remained, trying to keep themselves fit and occupied (they played a lot of ice hockey) until May 1919, when they were ordered forward to Ekaterinburg, where they joined Knox's training team. A local newspaper in Omsk had the following to say about them:

> *They march – if march is the word – with the light feet of sportsmen. Excellently clothed, healthy, fresh. The faces of strong determined people, expressing the blood of a whole nation. All seem young and at the height of their strength. They give the impression of what we Russians call culture, and more, of freedom, simplicity and naturalness . . . The indistinct figure of literature is made manifest in these English soldiers, who know how to live and conduct themselves. So fresh, so affable, such good spirits, such strength of body and mind. Yes, a fine people – what a fine people the English are. These Hampshires make us feel that about them.*[13]

To say the least, in some quarters the English were clearly welcome. There were, however, many other nations involved in this extraordinary affair.

The Times History of the War records that in March 1919 the Allied forces in Siberia consisted of the following:

55,000	Czechs
12,000	Poles
4,000	Serbs
4,000	Rumanians
2,000	Italians
1,600	British
760	French
28,000	Japanese
	[later increased to 70,000 – Author's note]
7,500	Americans
4,000	Canadians

Virtually all these contingents had different orders from their respective Governments. There was no clear agreed hierarchy of command and there were vast misapprehensions of what was actually happening in Siberia. It is not surprising that the joint venture, if these words can be used in this context, was to end in ignominious failure.

The young Horrocks (later a well-known general in the Second World War) of the Middlesex Regiment had been wounded and captured at Ypres in October 1914. His many attempts at escape were foiled and he was not released until November 1918. During his time as a prisoner, however, he had acquired one useful attribute; at one stage being confined in a room with only one other British officer and fifty Russians, he had learnt Russian. When the War Office called for 'volunteers who had the language to go to Russia to help the White Armies in their struggle against the Bolsheviks, I immediately applied and was ordered to Siberia.'[14]

Arriving at Vladivostok which was 'swarming with Russian refugees, Cossacks, Khirghiz, Mongolians, Chinese, Japs, with a few Americans, British and French thrown in, the harbour was packed with ships bringing war material, most of it British, for the White Armies.' It was explained to Horrocks that Admiral Kolchak's forces had driven the Bolsheviks back from Siberia into Russia proper, but this had mainly been achieved with the help of the Czechs who, seeing that the war was over, very naturally wished to go home. It was the British task to train and equip anti-Bolshevik Russian forces raised in Siberia to take their place on the front. Together with a platoon of British soldiers and fourteen other Russian-speaking officers, Horrocks set off on a train with twenty-seven wagons full of shells. After an eventful journey along the Chinese Eastern Railway the train, still, remarkably, with its twenty-seven wagons of shells, arrived at Omsk on 27 May 1919. This journey of 3,000 miles had taken just over a month. The party were then sent 800 miles further on to Ekaterinburg. The task of the British Military Mission was to turn raw recruits into a brigade of four battalions of front line soldiers, of which each had about seven British officers and twenty senior NCOs:

When the first batch of recruits, some 2,500 strong, shambled into the barracks we could hardly believe our eyes. In front came the extremely smart band and drums of the Hampshire Regiment followed by the filthiest and most unkempt mass of humanity I have ever seen in my life. Many of them were without boots or hat and nearly all were carrying the most dreadful looking bundles which contained their worldly possessions. It was soon obvious that we had been allocated the dregs from all the call-up depots in Siberia. Thirty-one percent were subsequently discharged on medical grounds alone.[15]

Sergeant Jupe of the Hampshire Regiment[16] records that he was made a Platoon Commander of No.3 Battalion of the Anglo/Russian Brigade: 'a strenuous time drilling them and had to acquire Russian words of command besides supervising their feeding and checking their kit which had a strong tendency to disappear.'

Horrocks records that he became really fond of the Russian NCOs in his school. He enjoyed his time with them and found them 'a good and extremely tough bunch and very good natured, provided they were properly looked after. The Russian barrack rooms swarmed with women every night. At first we tried to prevent this influx, but eventually had to give it up provided the women had gone before morning.'

The British had a difficult time with the White Russian military authorities who resented their help, particularly when the Anglo/Russian brigade was so clearly superior to the other, rather ragged, formations. In practice the British/Russian brigade never went into action.

Meanwhile, the Middlesex Regiment remained in Omsk, while their commanding officer, Colonel Ward, went on a lecture tour of railway depots all over Siberia and even into European Russia, at the request of Admiral Kolchak, addressing large audiences, mainly of railwaymen, about the advantages of trade unions, how they should be established and what their tasks should be. This must have been very far outside Ward's terms of reference as a British Army officer, albeit a Member of Parliament. However, almost everything about the British and

Allied intervention into Russia was similarly very far from what now would be known as politically, or even militarily, correct. Ward and his battalion then left for Vladivostok.

The Prinkipo affair, mentioned in Chapter Two (page 40), had an appalling effect on the White morale. How could the anti-Bolshevik so-called allies even contemplate a meeting at which the Whites would be asked to sit down with their murderous blood-stained enemy? 'Kolchak is said not to have slept a wink since he heard about Prinkipo.'[17] Indeed, Kolchak's position became ever more precarious. The Czechs had deserted him, the Americans were not prepared to fight at all, the Canadians had fallen out, the French, Poles, Rumanians and Italians were all vanishing and the few British, as he saw it, were not really prepared to go into action on his behalf. His own troops, seeing the writing on the wall, were deserting and, politically, the Allies were not prepared to grant him full recognition as the Supreme Ruler in the whole of Russia. Kolchak admitted to Colonel Stephens of the *Manchester Guardian* on 24 November 1919 that 'only large-scale Japanese intervention could save the situation, but he thought that if Bolshevism was to be defeated at all, such a defeat could only be effected if brought about by the Russians themselves.'

He was right. His armies collapsed and he was eventually handed over by the Czechs to the Bolsheviks in Irkutsk and shot.

The Middlesex Regiment had already left Vladivostok and the last of the British battalions, the Hampshires, having left Omsk in May, departed on 1 November 1919. According to Peter Fleming, 'Several of the officers and men were in or near to tears as the troopship drew away from the shore, not due to remorse or compassion about what they were leaving behind, but due to the fact that quarantine regulations enforced at the last moment obliged them to leave behind the dogs that they had adopted.'[18]

In Vladivostok, before they left, the Hampshires were billeted in a barracks overlooking those of the US troops. As Sergeant Jupe put it, 'As we paraded daily in the early morning for physical drill we were intrigued to witness a contingent of Russian women leaving the American quarters. Our men began to wonder whether there was something to be said for the American way of life after all.' He added, 'and so, the expedition petered out in futility'.[19]

Company Sergeant Major Ivens, Royal Engineers, who had been in the British Railway Mission in Siberia, wrote to his uncle from Vladivostok on 23 November 1919.[20] He begins by sympathizing with his uncle's troubles in moving house, 'I know what furniture removals are.' He then goes on at length, in surrealist contrast, to describe the chaos in Vladivostok and the battle which raged around them (they had to remain neutral) between the government troops (presumably the remains of the White Army) and the insurgents (the Bolsheviks) which resulted in a temporary White victory:

> About 5 am the station was attacked and taken by government troops. The insurgents fought room by room and had to be got out by hand grenades and were brought over here in groups of six and seven for trial. The fighting ceased at 8 am. Eighteen of the insurgents were taken back to the station and shot. They were placed at the top of a staircase and shot, so that their bodies tumbled down the stairs one after another. I was able to get over to the scene of fighting immediately afterwards. The dead were lying thickly along the road, wharves and railway lines – about 500 bodies and the ghastliness of the whole thing is indescribable. The interior of the station was the worst and this actually ran with blood. The remainder of the prisoners taken were marched to a distant part of the harbour and shot with machine guns. Thus ended the Revolution of 17/18 November, the result of which will only be to create a thirst for vengeance on the part of sympathizers of the rebels who are in a majority and sow the seeds of a worse outbreak at some future date. What struck me most was that both government troops and insurgents were wearing British clothing and boots and firing British ammunition out of American rifles and Canadian machine guns. There you have in a nutshell the result of Allied help in Russia . . .
>
> I trust you are still in good health and feeling the benefit of the change of residence. Please give my love to Annie and aunts S and M if with you.

Horrocks had found himself on the rear-rear party, being left, together with another officer, as liaison officer with the White

Siberian Army which was fast collapsing. The two of them reached Omsk without much difficulty and joined up with thirteen officers and men from the British Railway Mission which had been attempting to bring some sort of order into the chaotic situation. They continued their retreat in a railway wagon but eventually had to continue by sleigh. It was extremely cold. They were then captured by the Bolsheviks near Krasnoyarsk on 7 January 1920 after retreating for six weeks.

At first Horrocks and the very mixed party he was with were allowed to fend for themselves in Krasnoyarsk and he, amazingly, took a job teaching English at a girls' school to earn some, very little, money. After nine weeks in Krasnoyarsk they were moved to Irkutsk, 600 miles to the east, where they stayed for two months. 'It was in Irkutsk that I met my first woman commissar. She was an awesome sight. Tougher than any man I've ever seen. Her hair cut short, a cigarette in the corner of her mouth, a skirt which hung round her like a sack and a large revolver fastened to her belt. I would rather have tackled six men commissars any day.'[21]

In fact, the party did not go to Vladivostok, but were turned round and travelled the 3,500 miles to Moscow, where he was incarcerated in prison with 456 other prisoners – '45 women, generals, politicians, admirals, thieves, counter-revolutionaries, speculators, ex ladies-in-waiting and prostitutes, all mixed up together'. They were saved from starvation by a French organization in Moscow, run by a Madame Charpentier and her two daughters. Suddenly they were told that they were to be exchanged and to return to Britain at once. They arrived in Finland on 29 October 1920, eighteen months after he had first landed in Vladivostok.

Some of Lieutenant Colonel Riviere's reminiscences when interviewed by the author appear in chapter one. He expanded on this in two articles in his regimental magazine.[22] He covers the situation in forthright style: 'General Knox was up-country with the Russian C in C and the base at Vladivostok was commanded by a Brigadier Blair, who [very surprisingly] had been allowed to bring his wife with him.' He goes on to explain how, when the Middlesex were withdrawn in early autumn

1919, there was no one left to guard the stores. There were, however, a number of German and Austrian prisoners of war who were starving. They were put in British uniforms, received rations and given cudgels for guard duties. Riviere goes on to mention the action between the Bolsheviks and the anti-Bolsheviks described by CSM Ivens. He ends by describing his extraordinary journey back down the Chinese Eastern Railway in a commandeered train, adding that they were accompanied by Mrs Blair, who took with her a large pet brown bear cub all the way from Vladivostok via Peking to Shanghai. The bear excited the local dogs when she chained it to the balcony rail of her room. There was considerable noise and the bear was presented to the Shanghai Zoo.

We might leave the last, perhaps a bit simplistic, word on the Allied intervention in Siberia to CSM Ivens; 'Had the Allies kept out (and kept Japan out) the Russians would have fought each other to exhaustion before now and would have turned, perforce, to their only salvation – work.'[23]

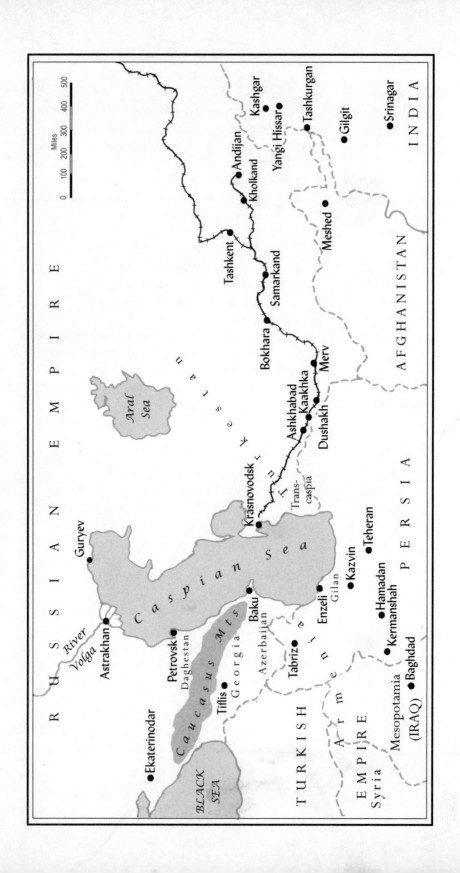

Chapter Five

THE CASPIAN AND
TRANSCASPIA

The Great Game between the British and the Russians during the late nineteenth and early twentieth century had provided many opportunities for dauntless young British and Russian officers to test their courage as they moved about the barren and often unknown lands to the north and north-west of India trying to secure ascendancy for their country in the face of enormous physical and other obstacles. There were, of course, other and more serious aspects to this situation. The Russians had been advancing into Turkestan since 1840 and by 1881 had annexed the entire Transcaspian region with its, to Western ears, highly romantic settlements of Bokhara, Samarkand and Tashkent. The Russians occupied Merv in 1884 and it began to look as if they would move in force into Afghanistan and perhaps even be poised for an onslaught into India. Then war with Germany began to loom and, very sensibly, both countries decided to settle their dispute, a peripheral matter when compared to the German menace. The Anglo-Russian Convention was signed in 1907, which effectively removed Russian influence from the area immediately bordering India. Persia was divided up between the two major powers as far as influence was concerned, with Britain getting the eastern region of the country and the whole of Afghanistan, while Russia was accorded sway in northern Persia. That was how matters were settled in those days.

With the onset of war, however, as far as the British hold on

India was concerned, the menace of the Russians was replaced by an arguably more sinister threat – the combined forces of Germany and Turkey, the latter with the great advantage of being a Muslim country with an obvious appeal to its fellow Muslims. The British defeat at Gallipoli had its repercussions in the east and north-east of Turkey and the fears of a Turkish move towards India became very real.

As long as Russia remained a combatant, the Turks were contained, but the second Russian Revolution and the resulting Russian armistice with Turkey in December 1917 removed the barrier which the Russians had been manning in northern Persia and the Turks began to move into the Caucasus. In fact, as a result of the Revolution, the three regions of the Caucasus – Georgia, Armenia and Azerbaijan – had declared their independence of Russia. The Turks, however, moved even further into the Caucasus with the intention of seizing the western and southern coasts of the Caspian Sea, rallying their fellow Muslims in the Caucasus, Transcaspia and Turkestan and threatening India. The Germans supported this move enthusiastically, with their eyes on the oil at Baku and other minerals and cotton in Transcaspia. In the chaotic situation of the time, the plan did not appear to be too far-fetched, certainly not to the British War Office, plagued as it was by many apparently insoluble problems on all sides.

The first idea to be produced by the military planners was for the Japanese to intervene in Siberia and move to Transcaspia to meet the Turks. A general staff memorandum of 25 March 1918 produced the following nightmare:

> *If German agents had free access to the lawless tribes of Afghanistan and the frontiers of India, bred as they had been on tales of a legendary wealth of loot which might be theirs, innumerable hordes of savage warriors would swarm into the plains, ravaging, murdering, destroying. The institutions built by long years of careful government would be swept away in a few short weeks and the attenuated garrison of the country would have to be largely reinforced from troops badly needed elsewhere. None but the White troops could be trusted.[1]*

The Chief of the Imperial General Staff added to this traumatic scene in a memorandum to the War Cabinet entitled *British Military Policy 1918–19* in the following terms,

> *Unless by the end of the war democratic Russia can be reconstituted as an independent military power it is only a question of time before most of Asia becomes a German colony and nothing can impede the enemy's progress towards India, in defence of which the British Empire will have to fight at every disadvantage.*[2]

The absurd notion of transporting a Japanese Army across Siberia and thence to Transcaspia with all its insuperable problems of supply, quite apart from the fact that the Japanese had absolutely no intention of doing anything of the sort, was quickly shelved, as were similar plans elsewhere. Three other ventures were eventually decided upon – the first to be known as Dunster Force, named after Major General Dunsterville (incidentally a school friend of Kipling and the original Stalky of *Stalky and Co*), which was sent up from Baghdad with the original objective of preventing the Turks from moving through the Caucasus. The second, some time after the creation of Dunster Force, was the despatch of Major General Malleson, an Indian Army Intelligence Officer of considerable experience, to Meshed in north-eastern Persia with the eventual aim of preventing the Turks from using the Transcaspian railway. Lastly, there was the sending of a Mission to Tashkent, initially under Sir George McCartney, with the objective of establishing exactly what was going on in the Turkestan area and, in so far as possible, trying to circumvent the seizure of the large stocks of cotton, used for the manufacture of guncotton, by Turkey or Germany and, furthermore, to prevent the disruption of Afghanistan by the Turks, Germans, and, later, the Bolsheviks. Luckily we have memoirs of all three leaders.[3]

Dunsterville had been commissioned in the Royal Sussex Regiment but, when in India had transferred to the Indian Army, to the 24th Punjabis. He had qualified in Urdu, Punjabi, Pushtu and Persian and, furthermore, was an interpreter in Chinese

103

and Russian. He also spoke French and German, a similar range of languages as those spoken by Ironside in the north. He was a man of commanding presence and great charm. On 24 December 1917, when in India, he was told of his appointment as 'Chief of the British Mission to the Caucasus and British representative in Tbilsi (Tiflis)'. Having arrived at Baghdad, he was told that he would be allocated 150 officers and 300 NCOs supported by five squadrons each of eight armoured cars and he was to proceed to Tiflis via Enzeli, on the southern shores of the Caspian, and Baku. His task was to organize and train Georgian, Armenian and Azerbaijani troops in order to resist the expected Turkish and German advance. His force began to arrive slowly in dribs and drabs and he decided to push ahead to Baku where he hoped to establish his, rather sketchy, command. Leaving Baghdad on 27 January 1918 with eleven officers, four NCOs and a few batmen(!) he hoped to reach Baku in about twelve days.

After the Revolution most of the Russian Army in Persia had returned home but a force under the anti-Bolshevik General Bicherakov had remained, its soldiers fiercely loyal to their commander and prepared to do anything he demanded of them. Dunsterville entered into a kind of alliance with him. There were, however, other elements on or about the makeshift snowbound road over the mountains to Enzeli, who were not at all enthusiastic about the British presence. The people of the district of Gilan with forces (known as the Jangalis or, by the British, Junglis, since part of their territory was covered by jungle) led by the formidable Mirzu Kuchik Khan were fiercely patriotic and anti-British and were determined not to let these 'foreigners' through their country. In this they were supported by the Bolsheviks who were in control of the port of Enzeli and were highly suspicious of British intentions. Dunsterville, with his tiny force, however, was able to bluff his way through and arrived at Enzeli on 17 February. He quickly realized that he and his party were in imminent danger of arrest. He managed to get away during the night and, after a few hiccups, he arrived at Kasvin and thence to the sizeable town of Hamadan. Although Bicherakov and his force were in control at Kermanshah,

Dunsterville's position was, at this time, extremely insecure. He asked for reinforcements and on 3 April twenty-seven more British officers and twenty more NCOs appeared, together with thirty soldiers of the 1st/4th Hampshire Regiment and one aeroplane – the latter a great propaganda coup.

Dunsterville's problems were exacerbated when Hamadan was affected by famine. There was food available but at a very high price and the local people could not afford to buy it. Many people were dying of starvation and there was some cannibalism. Dunsterville was able to institute famine relief and, before long, virtually all his force was employed on this task until the harvest came along, when conditions greatly improved. Dunsterville's position improved even more when a squadron of the 14th Hussars arrived. However, there was, in reality, nothing to stop the Turks from moving south-east from Tabriz and thence to Teheran, but he was able to deter any such move by the Turks using a mixture of bluff and rumour, vastly exaggerating the size of his still very small force.

The Bolsheviks were in control of Baku but were in difficulties with large sections of the population who resented their high-handed actions and attitudes. At one point Dunsterville had offered to help them against the Turks – a bizarre event if it had taken place – at the same time as the British were fighting the Bolsheviks in many places elsewhere. However, on 26 July a coup took place in Baku, the Bolsheviks were ousted and replaced by a 'Central Caspian Dictatorship' which requested Dunsterville's help. This whole idea was very much resisted by General Marshall, in command in Mesopotamia, and the same attitude of great reluctance to commit British troops on the western shores of the Caspian was taken by the authorities in London. However, Dunsterville's plea for permission to move to the support of those in Baku who were resisting the Turks was eventually agreed in London and reinforcements were despatched from Baghdad in the form of 39 Brigade, consisting of the 7th North Staffordshire Regiment, the 7th Gloucestershire Regiment, the 9th Royal Warwickshire and the 9th Worcester Regiment, all seriously below strength. They were also joined by two squadrons, each of sixteen armoured cars, from what had been the Russian Armoured Car Division of the Royal Naval Air Service, under the command of the remarkable Commander Locker Lampson, which had fought against the Austrians for the Tsar's and, later, for Kerensky's armies. Much of its fighting had been done in Rumania where it had earned a formidable reputation. After the second Revolution it had returned to England and had been absorbed into the Army, Locker Lampson being relieved of his command. The two squadrons which joined Dunsterforce had an epic journey over the mountains and remained with the Force throughout.[4]

Dunsterville's way to Enzeli, however, was still barred by the Jangalis, then under the command of a German officer. This force was eventually defeated and sued for peace. At this stage Enzeli was still under the control of the Bolsheviks. The arrival of Dunsterville and his force, however, changed this situation and control, in effect, passed to the British.

Dunsterville had been able to get hold of three steamers in Enzeli on payment – the *President Kruger* (1,000 tons), the *Kursk* and the *Abo*. Detachments from 39 Brigade began to move to Baku on 5 August 1918 and Dunsterville himself sailed for that port on the *Kruger* on 16 August. There had been a dispute as to which flag should be flown. Dunsterville had refused to fly the red flag and a compromise had been agreed to fly the Russian flag upside down – virtually no one realizing that this was in fact the flag of Serbia. As he put in his book:

> *Here is a flash in the blackness through which we were stumbling. A British General on the Caspian, the only Sea unploughed before by British keels, on board a ship named after a South African Dutch President and whilom enemy, sailing from a Persian port, under the Serbian flag, to relieve from the Turks a body of Armenians in a revolutionary Russian town. Let the reader pick his way through that delirious tangle, and envy us our task who will! . . . It took us some little time to understand the system of command on board a revolutionary ship. The arrangement was that all movements, and the general affairs of the ship, were run by a ship's committee of which the Captain was an ex officio member. In theory this was absurd; in practice we found that the crew were very amenable.[5]*

There were even further complications he might have mentioned. There were some 20,000 German and Austrian ex-prisoners whose one purpose was to return home and many of whom were being recruited into various armies – the Bolshevik, the Turkish, the Jangoli and the anti-Bolshevik Bicherakov armies – all with the same purpose in mind.

The problem with the defence of Baku was that the bulk of the defenders, mainly Armenian but with some Tartars and Russians, were not really prepared to fight: furthermore, in various degrees, they hated each other. The Bolshevik leaders had been arrested by the so-called committee, which called itself the government, and which spent most of its time holding meetings consisting of interminable arguments on irrelevant issues without ever coming to a clear-cut decision on anything. In theory Baku was run by five 'Dictators' who disagreed on almost everything except extreme disappointment that the British had not sent more troops.

The Adjutant of the North Staffordshire Regiment explained:

The factors in the situation were as follows:

1. *The wishes of Georgia, Armenia and Azerbaijan for independence*

2. *The wish of the Turks to have a good bargaining position, who at that stage had decided that they were going to lose the war and wished to grab as much of northern Persia as they could for barter purposes at the peace conference*

3. *The German wish to get across the Caspian Sea in order to get help for their tottering economy in food, wool, oil and manganese*

4. *The German wish to get through the North-West Frontier of India*

5. *The British wish to foil the Germans in all those aims*

6. *The Bolshevik wish to Bolshevise as much of Russia and Persia as possible.*[6]

A priority for Dunsterville was the arming of some merchant ships in order to protect his flanks and to secure his retreat, should that become necessary. A Commander Norris was sent from Baghdad with two officers and about thirty men. He had one 4" gun and two twelve pounders and other stores which were sent from Bombay for the purpose of arming further commandeered shipping. Difficulties with the so-called Dictators and the imminent Turkish attack, however, prevented any work being done in Baku and the arming of steamers did not really begin until Baku was evacuated and the British base was transferred to Enzeli.[7]

The Bolshevik commissars in Baku under their leader Schaumian tried to escape by ship with a considerable quantity of military stores, but this, somewhat surprisingly, was prevented by the anti-Bolshevik Russian Navy. The Bolshevists were allowed to leave by ship later but finished up in Krasnovodsk, where the anti-Bolsheviks were in full control, the episode ending in the famous execution of the twenty-six commissars to be dealt with later.

The main Turkish attack on Baku came on 26 August 1918. The Turks were vastly superior in numbers, the Armenians did not put up much resistance and, in spite of valiant efforts by 39 Brigade, it appeared that Baku was to fall very shortly. After interminable meetings of the so-called Baku Government, at which everyone present was allowed to speak at great length, long letters were written to Dunsterville imploring him to produce more troops, which he clearly could not do. An example of the kind of rubbish he had to endure follows. This was the last, and fourteenth, paragraph of a letter:

> In conclusion we beg to point out that the Dictatorship has no intention whatever "to command your detachment" or to influence military operations. The Dictatorship of the Centro-Caspia and Ispolkom (Executive Committee) represents the supreme power in Baku, pending the assembling of the Baku Council of Workmen, Soldiers' and Sailors' Deputies, and has appointed suitable and trained specialists (the Commander of the Force and the Chief of the Staff at the front and the Military and Naval Commissary at the rear) to the office of directing the fighting forces, to whom is entrusted control of the military operations of the Army and who, we trust, with your direct co-operation will

carry out firmly and energetically the only military demand of the Dictatorship, viz: the defence of the town at all costs from the Turks, until such time as the necessary reinforcements are forthcoming, whether from your side or other parts of Russia, and thus strengthen the common fighting front of the Allies against the armies of the Turko-German coalition. (signed President of the Dictatorship: H Tushoff, Vice President, members and secretary). (signatures illegible)[8]

Eventually, on 14 September, Dunsterville gave the order to withdraw. The Dictators told him that if he did so his ships would be fired upon by Russian ships under their control and, in particular, by the guard ship at the entrance to the harbour. In tense silence at night, four ships cast off and made for the open sea – the *Kruger* with the bulk of the troops on board, the *Kursk* and the *Abo* with the wounded, and a small steamer of 200 tons, the *Armenian*, with the bulk of the ammunition. As the *Kruger* left, a Russian sailor rushed on deck shouting that his wife had been left behind. The Russian crew insisted on turning round. The ship did so and she was picked up. The *Kruger* then left again but the same thing happened with another sailor. In the end, miraculously, all four ships got clear without any casualties and managed to reach Enzeli.

On 16 September Dunsterville was recalled to Baghdad. Before leaving he read to the assembled officers and men a petition which had been presented to him by the Russian crew of the *Kursk*. It read:

We, the Committee and the crew of the ss Kursk have witnessed with intense admiration the heroic conduct of your brave British soldiers in the defence of Baku. We have seen them suffering wounds and death bravely in the defence of our town which our own people were too feeble to defend. It is wonderful to us that these fine fellows from that distant island of the North Sea should have come all this way to the Caspian Sea and have given up their lives in the cause of honour and glory. We are so much impressed by their bearing and valour and by the whole episode of the British endeavours to save Baku from the Turks that we wish to be taken over as a body and granted British nationality.

The casualties of the British had been very high, the North Staffordshire Regiment suffering the greatest losses. Of the twenty officers and 480 men who fought there, eight officers and sixty-three men were killed, five officers and eighty men wounded, two officers and nineteen men subsequently died in Persia and forty more were evacuated sick to Enzeli. The British force had totalled 900, with about 8,000 local Russians of whom only 1,000 were at all reliable. On 15 September Azerbaijani troops entered Baku, the Turks holding back. The Armenia National Council announced later that 9,000 Armenians in the town were massacred.[9]

In fact, no oil from Baku got beyond Tiflis before the Turks signed an armistice on 31 October and the Germans on 11 November 1918.

After the armistice with the Turks, the British were told to re-occupy Baku. One thousand, two hundred British and 800 Indian troops landed there under Major General Thompson. Leslie Missen described life in Baku as follows:

> We really had a very pleasant time. The Opera House was re-occupied and we saw performances every fortnight. We were not allowed to carry arms and were supposed to be neutral between the various factions in the town. We lived on black bread, fresh fish and caviar, which our soldiers would not eat. We did, however, get some watermelons up from Enzeli.[10]

Paymaster Commander Franks describes how he arrived in Baku from Bombay on 6 January 1919 with the task of organizing the paying of the Russian crews the British were using for their purposes and for all work on the dockyard.[11] He had to deal with four different currencies – Baku Bonds, Kerensky and Nicolai (Tsarist) Notes and the Persian currency, all of which were based on the Rupee. He said it was, and no doubt this is true, extremely hard work. He did, however, find time to take Russian lessons with a charming Russian lady and to go a series of parties. He describes a Russian dinner party in the following terms: 'I arrived at 10.30 pm and we talked and drank until midnight. Then started Zakuski (small eats) still standing with a glass of vodka.

110

Then we began dinner proper at about 1 am. There were six courses with a toast after every course. Then we went to the drawing room where a small boy played a piano followed by a proper pianist. We began to dance while drinking more until 5.30 am.'

Under the command of Commander Norris and later, after Norris had an accident, Captain Washington, great activities took place in the dockyards at Enzeli re-arming and re-fitting the ships with guns and material which it was now possible to bring from the Black Sea by rail, and after the capture of the Russian flotilla, arming such captured ships as were considered useful. By the beginning of May fifteen ships were commissioned or about to be commissioned.[12] A number of naval actions took place against Bolshevik ships and the British-controlled Navy gradually obtained total domination of the whole of the Caspian Sea.

On 5 March 1919 Winston Churchill introduced the Army estimates into Parliament. He said:

> *The Admiralty have a fleet of armed vessels on the Caspian which gives us command of that extensive inland sea. The Bolsheviks have admitted the loss of five armed vessels. The personnel for these vessels commanded by the British reached the Caspian from Mesopotamia via Persia. The steamers are manned by Russians but the Commander and second-in-command are British as also are the gun crews. Each ship is supplied with an interpreter. The vessels are small and some carry only one gun of 4" calibre. The original Russian flotilla comprising two gunboats, two despatch vessels and three steamers were taken over by the British only a few days ago.*

Wing Commander Bowhill of 62 Wing Royal Air Force in the Caspian Sea reported[13] that from January to July 1919 his wing undertook the following operations:

> *For the Navy* – *reconnaissance and the bombing of the Bolshevik fleet, Astrakhan and all naval bases in the Volga delta.*
> *For the Army* – *reconnaissance and demonstration flights over the towns and villages of Daghestan, in order to keep the populace in order.* [a demanding and surprising task]

For the Russian Volunteer Army – *bombing and shooting up Bolshevik forces to the north of the Ekaterinador/Petrovsk railway and helping them in their advance to Astrakhan.*

All, however, was not plain sailing. Lieutenant Snow of the Royal Naval Reserve wrote to his mother on 2 January 1919 from Baku:

This is a dickens of a job we've taken on. The reconstruction of Russia. They don't want to be reconstructed. However, they have got to be, so they may as well settle down to it. He goes on, I am in command of a ship – Allah Vardi or, in English, God's gift. There is only one thing to recommend her – she has the luck of Old Nick himself. The crew is Russian. There are six Russian officers, myself and one other British officer. These perishing people know that the rumour has got around that we are going home, are beginning to appreciate us and are all for trying to persuade us to stop. But as far as I am concerned, I'd see em in the remotest part of Hades before I voluntarily stay one hour in their beastly country.[14]

Mr Lambert, the former Civil Lord of the Admiralty, wrote an article in the *Daily Sketch* on 13 March 1919, 'A fleet in the Caspian Sea to put down Bolshevism is like an excursion to the zoo to tackle a rhinoceros with a feather.'

Air Vice Marshal Bilney[15] describes how, after the armistice, volunteers were called for to join the 'Army of Occupation in South Russia [sic]'. He arrived at Petrovsk, a port north of Baku, on 1 March 1919 where he found that the occupying force consisted of one company of Punjabis, relieved later by Gurkhas. The RAF wing consisted of 221 Squadron of DH9, later DH9A, day bombers. It was his job to prepare for the arrival of a seaplane squadron. The conditions in the town were very unsettled. The atrocities on both sides were terrible (this is a constant refrain throughout the affair in southern Russia). The personnel of 266 (seaplane) Squadron arrived in early April. There was a tragedy when two Royal Marines got hold of a jar of Navy rum, one of them dying. Bilney was posted to command a flight of seaplanes. At first they found great difficulties in taking off because it had not been realized that the effect of the fresh water in the Caspian was greatly to reduce buoyancy when compared to sea water and the seaplanes had to be modified.

The Bolsheviks still had three destroyers in the Volga estuary near the town of Guryev on the north shore of the Caspian Sea. It was thought that the people in that town were anti-Bolshevik and had some military personnel. Bilney was deputed to command a detachment of three officers and some maintenance personnel to train these anti-Bolshevik aviators how to fly seaplanes – a 'very strange mission', as he put it. The Caspian was very shallow in that area and he, with one seaplane, was let down from the seaplane carrier some thirty miles offshore. He landed near the town to find that no one had the remotest idea of why he was there or what he was supposed to be doing. Furthermore, no one spoke English. Eventually, however, he did find one man who did, who happened to be the son of the composer Rachmaninov. He managed to teach a few Russians the rudiments of seaplane flying, but eventually he was recalled when one of the aircraft, while being piloted by a Russian on a bombing raid, blew up. He discovered that the Russian idea of bombing was for the pilot to carry a bomb in his lap, pull out the safety pin and drop it on the target. Obviously something had gone very wrong.

Before he left he was inaugurated as a Cossack at an extremely drunken party from which he did not recover for a week.

There were a number of Bolshevik-inspired strikes in 1919 in all the ports on the Caspian where the British were based and, as usual, the Bolsheviks tried to subvert the British servicemen, with scant success.

One example was kept by Sub Lieutenant Grundy. It read as follows:

COMERADS BRITISH SOLDIERS!

We congratulate you with great international workmen holliday- the first of May. To day for workmen of all parts of world is great holliday.

Comerads soldiers of British troops!! The great war of im- perialists continued 5 ears finished, and now people of all countries strugle against its own government and against rich classes. The firs, who has distroyed the power of its government

and rich class is Russian workmen and peasants. They coll now
workmen of all the world to go against all the kings all the rich
class.

Germany, Austria folowed our example. Workmen of These
countries have no more Imperialistic government, they have
Consills of workmen, peasant and soldiers deputles.

Great batlle between imperialistic rich class and peasants
began.

With Russian workmen, workmen of England, Germany,
France, Austria, America yon must coll to-day.

Behind international imperialism!

Be a life international revolution of workmen!!

Be a life third international of communism!!

Be a life general Union of Sovetrepublic of World!!

Be a life British Socialistic Republic,

Be a life the Russian bolchevic party.

Comitee of Russian Communist Party of Baku.[16]

It is perhaps not surprising that the British soldiers, sailors and airmen were not totally convinced.

As well as controlling the ports of Enzeli, Baku and Petrovsk, the British managed to secure the important port of Krasnovodsk which became one of the keys to Major-General Malleson's operations in Transcaspia. Eventually, of course, the British had to withdraw. As Commander Norris put it:

We started with a small party of twenty-two men. We were
besieged in Baku and had to evacuate. We started afresh to arm
the ships. The Army was conveyed back to Baku, which place was
re-occupied. The Bolsheviks were prevented from reinforcing
their base south of the winter ice, and that base was bombarded
and burnt. The squadron grew to nine armed ships, four carriers
and twelve coastal motor boats, and our numbers were about
twelve hundred officers and men of the Royal Navy and Royal
Air Force. We gradually got better guns, though these did not
come until nearly the end. We never got over the boiler trouble,
but we did manage to keep at sea. Baku was never threatened.
The Bolsheviks, when they came out of the Volga, were given a
good thumping, and had to go home again. Finally, we covered
the evacuation from Baku and came away ourselves.[17]

Malleson's Military Mission arrived in Meshed in Persia in the middle of July 1918. Malleson had been told that his objective was 'To check as far as possible the Turkish and German designs to penetrate via Baku and Krasnovodsk with the active or tacit consent of the Bolsheviks, then in control of Turkestan, to the Afghan frontier where their object was to bring pressure to bear on Afghans and tribesmen alike to embark on a religious war against the British in India.'[18] For this formidable task he was originally given the help of one British officer, shortly augmented by several additional Russian and Persian-speaking officers and a small detachment of Indian troops from units stationed in the Persian province bordering India.[19]

The contrast between Malleson's and Dunsterville's personalities was very great: Dunsterville a leader to his fingertips; Malleson a dour, prickly, introverted man with few leadership qualities but with exceptional talents as an Intelligence Officer – he had been on the Intelligence staff of the Indian Army continually from 1904.

After the Revolutions the Bolsheviks had assumed control of the whole of Transcaspia. In spite of a pronouncement by Lenin promising autonomy to the peoples of Turkestan, the Bolshevik authorities based in Tashkent were treating them in an appallingly high-handed and often bloodthirsty manner. Indeed, it seemed to many of the tribesmen of Russian Turkestan that the Bolsheviks, far from bringing liberation from the Tsarist rule under which they had been suffering, were in fact far worse. There was general dissatisfaction, resulting in demonstrations at Ashkhabad and elsewhere. Frolov, a Bolshevik Commissar from Tashkent, was sent to Ashkhabad to pacify the locals. He arrested and shot a number of the railway workers' leaders. But hatred of the Bolshevik rule was such that it was not long before he, together with his bodyguard and others, were themselves murdered. This led to a general rising along the whole of the Krasnovodsk/Merv railway and a socialist/revolutionary government was established with its headquarters at Ashkhabad which, having shot all the Bolshevik Commissars it could find, shortly controlled the whole railway line from Krasnovodsk to Merv. Similar events took place at Bokhara, where a Bolshevik delegation arrived to see the Emir and were very quickly dealt with, the leader of the delegation being thrown to the ground from the top of a minaret.

It was evident that it would not be long before the Bolshevik Government in Tashkent would counterattack with its 'Red' armies. Malleson had an extremely efficient intelligence organization throughout Transcaspia and had been keeping in close touch with the situation. The Ashkhabad Committee, only too aware of its weakness, appealed to him for military help.

Malleson's resources were very slender. There were a few troops in eastern Persia including the 28th Light Cavalry and the 19th Punjabis, together with a few men in Meshed. He asked the authorities in India for permission, if necessary, to send troops to support the Ashkhabad Committee and, without any authorization from Whitehall, he was given a free hand by the Commander-in-Chief, General Monro, to do as he thought fit. He then sent a liaison officer, Captain Teague-Jones, to negotiate with the Ashkhabad Committee. The result was an agreement whereby, in return for help in the defence of the port of Krasnovodsk and, if necessary, for making the Transcaspian railway inoperable, the British would supply some limited military assistance to the sorely pressed Ashkhabad force which was commanded by Oraz Sirdar, a Turkman officer of the Tsarist Army who, like many of his compatriots, had decided that his hatred of the Bolsheviks was greater than his dislike of the Ashkhabad Committee.

On 10 August the first British led troops, in fact a company of infantry and machine-gun section of the Indian Army, crossed the frontier and went up the railway line in order to assist Oraz Sirdar in consolidating a new position. Reinforcements in the form of the second and third companies of the 19th Punjabis soon arrived and after a fierce action at Kaakhka, during which a company of Punjabis charged with fixed bayonets, the Red forces were defeated and retired in disorder. The small British/Indian force suffered a high percentage of casualties – three officers and twenty-four soldiers being killed or wounded. Further reinforcements – a company of the 1st/4th Hampshire Regiment and a battery of the 44th Royal Field Artillery

Regiment arrived a few days later, followed on 25 September by two squadrons of the 28th Cavalry.

On 16 September the news that Baku had fallen to the Turks arrived at Meshed and Ashkhabad. This created some apprehension in Meshed that the small British force now strung out along the Central Asian railway was becoming highly vulnerable: there was near panic in Ashkhabad.

Shortly afterwards, Malleson was informed that a party of Bolshevik commissars let by Schaumian, the previous head of the Bolshevik Baku government, had landed at Krasnovodsk and had been arrested (see page 108). In fact they had set off in a ship bound for the Bolshevik-held port of Astrakhan but the Captain and sailors of the vessel had decided that it was safer for them to take the commissars to Krasnovodsk. The Ashkhabad Committee at Krasnovodsk was fearful that the arrival of the commissars would spark off a Bolshevik rising in the whole of Transcaspia and, through an emissary, asked Malleson what they should do with their captives. Malleson says that he replied that the prisoners should be handed over to him to be held as hostages for the release of British people under arrest by the Soviet Government and that he sent a telegram to Teague-Jones, informing him of the position.

The Ashkhabad Committee met the same night in order to come to a decision about the commissars. Teague-Jones was present, but left after midnight, having been told that the decision would not be taken that night. The Committee Chairman, Funtikof, was drunk and Teague-Jones apparently saw no point in remaining. The next morning he managed to approach Funtikov, who was still drunk and, to his dismay, was told that the commissars had all been shot. In fact they had been taken by train towards Ashkhabad, told to get out and summarily shot on the spot. Initially the news was not released but it was not long before the truth got out. The Bolshevik government in Moscow used it in a major anti-British and highly effective propaganda drive, throughout the area and indeed the world, stating as a fact that Malleson had ordered the executions and that Teague-Jones had actually given the order and had been present at the event. A picture, which became famous, was painted of the executions, with Teague-Jones in a prominent position. There was no truth in these allegations but the mud did stick for some considerable time and, indeed, Teague-Jones had to change his name for fear of assassination.

Teague-Jones apparently took the name of Ronald Sinclair and never revealed his true identity. After his death on 16 November 1988, however, an obituary appeared in *The Times* (23 November) which disclosed the truth and the fact that he had published a travel book in his 100th year under his assumed name. A book was published by Gollanz in 1990,– *The Spy who Disappeared, Diary of a Secret Mission to Russian Central Asia in 1918*. This is said to be based on Teague-Jones's diaries and a journal which he wrote in 1920. As far as the murder of the twenty-six Commissars is concerned, it varies somewhat from the official version above. Malleson and Colonel Ellis (an Australian officer on Malleson's staff at Meshed) reported, as stated above, that Malleson asked for the twenty-six Commissars to be handed over to him. Teague-Jones (if the book is wholly authentic) states that Malleson had told the Ashkabad Committee 'that it was very difficult to find the necessary guards to send them down to India and suggested that the Transcaspian authorities should find some other way of disposing of them.

The one certainty in this murky business is that Malleson did not order the Commissars to be shot and Teague-Jones was certainly not present at the executions.

Malleson now decided to attack and a major, but inconclusive, action took place at Dushakh. The British and Indians, however, suffered very heavy casualties. The 19th Punjabis lost all their British officers killed or wounded and forty-seven killed and 139 wounded among other ranks. The 28th Cavalry lost six killed and eleven wounded. The Transcaspian forces lost seven killed and thirty wounded. The Red Army lost at least 1,000 killed and wounded.[20] The Transcaspian force, and in particular the Turkoman Cavalry, were most unreliable and, as always seemed to be the case, it was the British and Indian forces who did most of the fighting; indeed, the Indian Army achieved an almost mythical status of invincibility in the minds of the Bolshevik soldiers, who promptly withdrew beyond Merv which was occupied by the British Transcaspian force at the end of October 1918, after which winter set in and hostilities between the British/Transcaspian and the Red Armies died down.

Long before the collapse of Turkey and the armistice of November 1918, therefore, any pretence that the British interest in Transcaspia was primarily aimed at preventing a German/Turkish advance to India had vanished. The enemies of the British were the Bolsheviks, and that was that.

Malleson was now given firm instructions not to advance beyond Merv. The authorities in both India and Whitehall were becoming concerned about the position of British forces deep in Transcaspia in support of a very shaky Ashkhabad Committee. Much to Malleson's delight, in January 1919 his Mission passed from the control of the Commander-in-Chief in India to that of General Milne at Constantinople, who, unlike the hierarchy in India, actually visited Malleson, who had by that time established his headquarters at Ashkhabad, and made a tour of the area. Malleson had had a bad relationship with the Indian authorities. In his lecture he spoke of his bosses as, 'Some gentlemen in easy chairs on a hill top 2,000 miles away'. He went on, 'It was evident that we should not remain indefinitely in Turkestan. The British Army was being demobilized, the expenses were great and it was abundantly clear that the local inhabitants were quite content that we should do the fighting for them while they took their ease.'[21]

In February 1919 Malleson received the order that his force, now still under 1,000 strong, should evacuate the country forthwith. This, of course, meant almost certainly condemning the Transcaspian anti-Bolshevik forces to total disaster in the long term. Malleson asked if withdrawal could be postponed for a month or two and kept secret in the meantime. His expertise in intelligence work came to the fore and he managed to spread rumours to the effect that the British were in fact going to advance and that the apparent signs of withdrawal were merely a cover plan. He also managed, by spreading untrue rumours of the perfidy of each, to destroy the relationship between the Bolsheviks and the Afghans, which was beginning to become dangerous.

Eventually Malleson had to inform the Ashkhabad Committee of the impending British withdrawal. This was received with great consternation and impassioned pleas were made for its reversal. However, this was clearly impossible. A final hope for the Ashkhabad Committee was that Denikin's forces in the North Caucasus, which had succeeded in occupying Petrovsk, north of Baku, would send troops to prop up their situation. Several hundred infantry and artillery troops did arrive, but the general atmosphere in Ashkhabad became more and more apathetic and gloomy. The last engagement between British troops and the Red Army took place on 2 March and all British and Indian soldiers had left Transcaspia by 1 April 1919. The naval base at Krasnovodsk remained in British hands for several months.

A considerable quantity of military stores was left behind for the use of the Ashkhabad Committee, but, without the opposition of the British, the Red advance was remorseless. Merv was occupied in May, Ashkhabad in July and, the British having left for Enzeli, Krasnovodsk fell in January 1920.

While all this was taking place, the British had not been inactive in Tashkent.

If anything, the situation in Russian Turkestan had been more chaotic than that in Transcaspia. Of a total population of seven million, ninety-five per cent were native Mohammedans and five per cent European Russians. Under the Tsars the European Russians had provided the government and commanded the Army. After the Revolution the Turkestan people thought that the various pronouncements in favour of self-determination, both by Kerensky's government and later by Lenin, must apply to them. They were sorely mistaken. After the second Revolution the Bolsheviks took control of Turkestan. A self-proclaimed independence government of Mohammedans at Kolkhand was attacked by the Red Army. Thousands were massacred and many mosques were destroyed. A further bloody revolt was crushed by the Bolsheviks in January 1918. But no one knew what policies the Bolsheviks in central Asia would adopt. Their links to Moscow were, at best, tenuous and most of the leaders were without even primary education and completely unversed in the art, or science, of government. There were two other complications. Stockpiled in the area were some 20,000 tons of raw cotton desperately needed by both sides in the war for the manufacture of explosives. There were also some 33,000 Austrian, Hungarian and German liberated prisoners of war who had survived the starvation and typhus which had taken a very heavy toll. In one barracks, all the prisoners, 280 in number, had died of typhus.[22] Many of the survivors had joined the Red Army, certainly partially in order to get food; indeed, some Red Army detachments were almost entirely composed of prisoners of war.

The British authorities both in London and India were virtually entirely ignorant of what was going on in the area. They were worried about German incursion into Afghanistan and India, and they decided to send a small Mission to Tashkent with the additional aim of trying to prevent any of the stockpiled cotton from reaching Germany. The most obvious starting point for this venture was Kashgar in Chinese Turkestan, where the British Consul General, Sir George McCartney, was just about to retire, to be replaced by a Major Etherton, from the Indian Army, author of the book *Through Mongolia*. The Mission consisted of Colonel Bailey, a well-known explorer in Tibet and south-west China, and Major Blacker of the Indian Guides, also a very experienced traveller in central Asia (later to become known as the first man to fly over Mount Everest and the inventor of the Blacker Bombard produced for the defence of Britain in the Second World War).

Bailey and Blacker set off for Kashgar from Srinagar in Kashmir, over the mountains, on 22 April 1918. They had a platoon of guides with them. As Blacker put it:

There were linguists, speakers of Russian, Turkish, Persian, Arabic and even French; a bomber, a machine gunner, a signaller, a carrier pigeon expert, two or three skilled topographers, scouts, a first aid man and a veterinarian, whilst practically every NCO carried on him the scars of a protracted sojourn on the Western Front and others had seen fighting in Africa, Persia and on the Afghan frontier.[23]

121

Blacker started off on a motor bicycle, the first to be seen in Sinkiang, a two-stroke Triumph:

> *We had prepared this with great care in the Rawalpindi Transport Depot. It was packed in five cases for manned porterage and fitted with an auxiliary tank so it might be seen as kerosene.*

Most of the guides travelled on yaks. The party crossed the Chinese border and reached Tashkurgan on 27 May. Continuing over the Pamirs with a small Chinese escort and struggling over passes of over 13,000 feet, they reached the town of Yangi Hissar, where they were given a tremendous reception by the Chinese who greeted them with banners and trumpeters, playing them through the beflagged streets. The remainder of the journey consisted of a number of similar receptions, concluding on 7 June with a ride through the streets of Kashgar, together with Sir George McCartney. The Chinese were clearly allies of Britain and the Imperial Russian representatives were still in situ in Kashgar. It was arranged that Bailey and Blacker should go to Tashkent, to be followed shortly by Sir George McCartney who would introduce them to the Bolshevik authorities with the objective of finding out what was going on – clearly a somewhat dangerous undertaking in the circumstances. McCartney arranged for Mr Stephanovitch, the Secretary of the Russian Imperial Consulate General in Kashgar, to go with them as pilot in China and, hopefully, help them across the Russian border. Mrs Stephanovitch was to, and did, accompany them, 'as she had shopping to do in Tashkent and wished to see a dentist', an almost surrealist touch.[24] In the event Mr Stephanovitch turned back, very wisely in the circumstances, shortly after crossing the Russian border, but his dauntless wife continued. They managed to get on a train at Andijan, in itself a considerable feat, and arrived in Tashkent on 14 August 1918, just under four months after leaving Srinagar: journeys were not quick in those days. The redoubtable Mrs Stephanovitch, apparently, did her shopping, saw her dentist and returned with Sir George McCartney a fortnight or so later.

According to Blacker[25], on the journey over the Pamirs, 'Our little army of sixteen was enlarged by popular report to 60,000.

This figure spread all over central Asia and caused some unease to our adversaries.'

It was most unfortunate that British and Russian, albeit Bolshevik Russian, troops had fired on each other in anger, for the first time since the Crimean War, at Ashkhabad just a few hours before Bailey and Blacker arrived. They knew nothing about this and were caught by total surprise when, at their first meeting with the Red Commissar for Foreign Affairs, they were confronted with this affair. Blacker, less scrupulous than Bailey, said that if the story was true the troops concerned must be former Indian Army soldiers who had hired themselves out to the anti-Bolsheviks as mercenaries. In fact, of course, as we have already noted, the troops concerned were under the command of Major General Malleson.

Sir George McCartney arrived in Tashkent on 24 August. On the surface life was not unpleasant. Although most hotels and restaurants were closed or turned into Soviet institutions and all cars had been commandeered for the use of Bolshevik officials, the theatre was still open and, perhaps the most extraordinary incident in the whole of this study, an Englishman passed through Tashkent with a troupe of performing elephants.[26] However, the situation was deteriorating fast as far as the British were concerned.

On 1 September McCartney, Bailey and Blacker were summoned to see Kolesof, an ex-Sergeant Major in the Tsarist Army, the Bolshevik President of the Republic and the most influential man in Russian Turkestan. McCartney explained the objective of the Mission, which was only concerned with the possible advance of the Germans to Baku and thence towards the Indian and Afghan frontiers. Somewhat to the Mission's surprise Kolesof ignored the happenings at Ashkhabad and concentrated on the British attack at Archangel which, he said, was tantamount to a declaration of war.[27] McCartney half-expected to be arrested and cast into jail but there was, temporarily, no such development and he left Tashkent for India via Chinese territory on 15 September 1918, taking with him Blacker, who was ill, and Mrs Stephanovitch, thus leaving Bailey in Tashkent alone.

123

Bailey was a most remarkable man, of infinite resource and courage, together with great experience of intelligence work in the area. He was also possessed of enormous charm. He struck up a great friendship with the American Consul, Tredwell. He also made friends with a Russian member of the Cheka, the notorious and terrifying Bolshevik Intelligence Organization, which was, then and later, responsible for thousands, if not hundreds of thousands, of executions of so-called enemies of the Soviet Union. Before long it became obvious that he was to be arrested and probably executed. He had managed to acquire an Austrian soldier's uniform. Wearing this disguise and with a false passport, he disappeared on 20 October. He was hidden in Tashkent by various friends at risk of certain death if they were discovered. Tredwell, the American Consul, was arrested on 26 October and suffered five months' internment before eventually being released.

After a week or so Bailey managed to get out of Tashkent and spent several months wandering across the mountains from one hiding place to another, sometimes on his own and sometimes in company of various assorted people, including an ex-Tsarist General Kondratovich, with the nickname of Garibaldi. After a series of hair-raising escapes he returned to Tashkent just after a failed revolution by anti-Bolsheviks headed by Ossipov, a youth of twenty-three, who had been the Bolshevik Commissar for War. As Bailey puts in his book:

> Ossipov went to the barracks of the 2nd Turkestan Regiment, telephoned the White House, the residence of Kolesof, the head of the Government, that there was trouble at the barracks and asked that some of the commissars would come and help him to settle it by talking to the men. Eight of them came . . . Ossipov shot the lot. He then declared that the Bolshevik regime was ended and proceeded to get drunk . . . After the conventional precaution of shooting all members of the Cheka who were at headquarters, one of the first things Ossipov did was to go to the bank and remove all the money.[28]

After some bitter fighting the Revolution was defeated. Ossipov fled and the Bolsheviks took fearful vengeance. About 4,000, including many whose sole crime was to wear a collar and were therefore 'bourgeois counter-revolutionaries', were shot.

Bailey, however, managed to avoid this, arriving in Tashkent some little time later. His previous objective had been to find out what support Malleson's small force with his anti-Bolshevik allies would get from the locals in the area when, as he expected, they advanced on Tashkent. However, hearing that Malleson's forces had, on orders from above, retired to Meshed, he realized that there was no reason for him to remain in Tashkent and decided to get out. He had been on the run for a year or more, assuming a number of different changes of identity. At one stage the hunt for him and others was so intense that he was forced to sleep in a different house every night: he had many very loyal friends.

Ultimately, with supreme daring, with an Albanian identity, he managed to get himself taken on as an agent by the Cheka with the purpose of getting into Bokhara, still an anti-Bolshevik enclave, in order to report on the rumour that British officers were training the Bokharan Army. Fifteen Cheka spies had been sent there for that purpose; all had been discovered and executed. Bailey was successful in entering Bokhara and, in a final irony, received a message from his Cheka bosses to the effect that he should look out for a notorious British spy – Colonel Bailey. Having divulged his true identity to the Emir, he set out for the 400-mile journey to Persia across the desert, with a party including seven White Russian officers, leaving on 18 December 1919. Seventeen months after leaving India, Bailey once more reached friendly soil. In fact he had achieved very little but his reappearance was greeted with great joy, the *Daily Telegraph* headlining it, 'British Officer in Bolshevik Asia . . . Amazing Adventure'.

An even more remarkable, but not publicized, story concerned one of those, now vanished, breed of women, a Miss Houston, a governess (of Irish stock). She worked for a Russian family named Noyev. She had three charges, two girls aged about fourteen and seven and a boy of about eight. The elder girl and the boy eventually became British subjects. The boy became an officer in the Royal Engineers and the girl was secretary to Edgar

Wallace up to the time of his death. Miss Houston somehow survived all the extraordinary and murderous events in Tashkent, giving Bailey continuous and effective help and finding havens and disguises for him. She would have been executed instantly had these activities become known to the authorities, but she remained calm and undaunted throughout. As private teaching was forbidden, she was forced to teach in a Soviet military school and managed to get herself transferred to Ashkhabad where she went into hiding. She then bribed a Persian to take her through the mountains to Persia. Mounted on a pony without a saddle for three days and sleeping in the open, she finally managed to get to Persia through the snow with a party of smugglers. She was an elderly lady. They made them tough in those days.

Chapter Six

THE CAUCASUS

We have seen how, after the Treaty of Brest-Litovsk, the Turks advanced across the Caucasus and eventually captured Baku on the Caspian Sea. As part of the armistice agreement on 31 October 1918 between the Turks and the Allies, the Turks agreed to withdraw all their troops from the Caucasus. There had been a secret agreement between France and Britain on 27 December 1917, negotiated in Paris without the knowledge of the Americans, under which anti-German and, later, anti-Bolshevist activities in the South of Russia were divided into areas of responsibility. The French were to be responsible for Bessarabia, the Ukraine and the Crimea while the British had the Cossack territories, the Caucasus, Armenia and Georgia. The British were therefore responsible for overseeing the Turkish withdrawal from the Caucasus and the 27th Division was sent there under the command of General Forestier Walker, with brigades at Batum, Tiflis and Baku.

Many of the troops, no doubt, had no idea why they were there. A flavour of the feelings of some of them comes from two communications sent to his mother by Lance Corporal Stell of C Company of the 8th Battalion Royal Fusiliers on 23 July 1919 from Tiflis. The first was on two postcards with pictures of Tiflis on the back. It read as follows:

Dear Mother, hope this card finds you all in the very best of good health as I am at present. The discipline here is absolutely hellish, we are having a dog's life and have been here three days and this is about the first opportunity I have had to write. We are cleaning

127

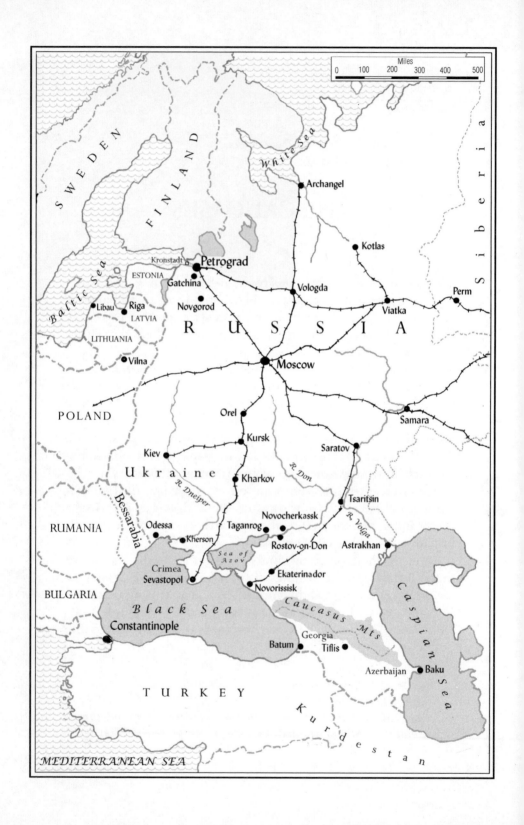

Miles
0   100   200   300   400   500

SWEDEN

FINLAND

White Sea

Archangel

Kotlas

Siberia

Perm

Kronstadt
ESTONIA
Petrograd
Gatchina
Baltic Sea
Libau   Riga
LATVIA
Novgorod
LITHUANIA
Vilna

Vologda

Viatka

R U S S I A

Moscow

POLAND

Orel

Kursk

Kiev

U k r a i n e

Kharkov

R. Dnieper

Samara

Saratov

R. Don

Tsaritsin

RUMANIA

Bessarabia

Odessa
Kherson

Taganrog

Novocherkassk

Rostov-on-Don

Sea of Azov

R. Volga

Astrakhan

BULGARIA

Crimea
Sevastopol

Ekaterinador

Novorissisk

Black Sea

Constantinople

Batum

Caucasus Mts

Georgia
Tiflis

Caspian Sea

Azerbaijan   Baku

TURKEY

K u r d e s t a n

MEDITERRANEAN SEA

and polishing all day long. We are not here to put down Bolshevism, but to guard British capital sunk in the extensing (sic) oil fields.[1]

The second card, about a month later on 26 August 1919, had on the front a picture of himself having his boots cleaned by a local. It read as follows;

I had this photograph taken today in the Botanic Gardens. This gives you an idea of the life we are living. We never clean our own boots for a bit of bread, a few scraps of bacon or any leavings at all we get our boots brushed. How do you like me in my sun toppy (sic). I had this photo taken while I waited. It is not bad at all but what do you think about it? Best love to you all at home. Sincerely. Fred.

Lance Corporal Stell clearly had changed his view about his situation in Tiflis during that month. However, the reasons why he was there were the occasion of long debate in the Eastern Committee of the War Cabinet which was set up by Lloyd George to deal with the mass of problems facing Britain in the Middle East and Persia. Its Chairman was Lord Curzon, who had been Viceroy of India and was Lord Privy Seal at the time, becoming Foreign Secretary on 29 October 1919. Its members were Jan Smuts, Lord Robert Cecil (Deputy to the Foreign Secretary, Balfour), Edwin Montague (Secretary of State for India) and Sir Henry Wilson (Chief of the Imperial General Staff).

Curzon told his Committee on 2 December 1918 that war had demonstrated that it was essential to the interests of the British Empire, and of India in particular, that Britain should exercise some measure of political control over Transcaucasia.[2] The presence there of military forces hostile to the British Empire would turn Britain's flank in Asia as it had so nearly been turned during the summer of 1918. Furthermore, disorder in the Caucasus would make the region an Asian Balkans. Any sort of anarchy, disorder or Bolshevism there would inevitably react upon the whole British position from Persia eastward. He went on to say that Batum must once again become a free port, the main outlet for the oil from Baku. 'The idea that the Azerbaijanis, the Armenians or the Bolsheviks could permanently hold Baku and control the vast resources there is one that cannot be entertained for a moment.'

In fact, these views were remarkably similar to Corporal Stell's initial views of the reasons for his presence in Tiflis.

Curzon's views, however, were not accepted then or later by the Eastern Committee. Montague asked, 'What is the point of it all? Why do we want to take any responsibility?' Cecil said that we should keep open the lines of communication to India. Why not give the job to the French? Smuts thought this was dangerous: 'France might one day be the British Empire's greatest problem.' America was suggested: 'they were perhaps less selfish than the French but would not be there for long.'

A paper was eventually produced by the General Staff which said:

> From the military point of view it would be most undesirable for the approaches to India from South Russia, the Black Sea and Turkey in Asia, which converge at Batum, to be placed at the disposal of an ambitious military power (France) which, although friendly to us at the moment, is our historical world rival. In fact it does not appear to the General Staff that any other power except herself can be permitted by Great Britain to function in this manner.

A later meeting was attended, unusually, by Balfour, the Foreign Secretary, who made the almost incredible point that he had never been consulted about sending a division to the Caucasus and was, 'much alarmed "when he learnt about it".'

The following remarks were then made:

> Mr Balfour – 'Of course the Caucasus would be much better governed under our aegis than it would be under French aegis. But why should it not be mis-governed?'
> Lord Curzon – 'That is the other alternative – let them cut each other's throats.'
> Mr Balfour – 'I am in favour of that.'[3]

The arguments in the Eastern Committee continued with the Secretary for India, Montague, arguing that as far as the defence of India was concerned, it did not seem, 'to me to be necessary for us to give a thought to the Caucasus'.

In the event the troops remained in the Caucasus; eventually two divisions were stationed there, some 40,000 men – far more than anywhere else on the periphery of the old Tsarist Russian state.

In a final twist to this extraordinary story, fed up with retaining two divisions of soldiers, many of whom were required elsewhere and some of whom should have been demobilized, the British Government suggested that the responsibility for the Caucasus should be handed to Italy, who looked at the oil deposits in Baku with longing eyes and, furthermore, who felt that it had been badly done by in the division of the spoils of war. The Italians agreed and plans were made for the hand-over. At this stage, however, the Italian Government fell and its successors cancelled the whole venture.

Once the Turks and Germans had been evacuated from the area, Major Generals Thomson and Forestier Walker at Baku and Tiflis respectively had been told that their mission was simply to guard the communications between the Black and Caspian Seas and that they were not to enter into the internal political or administrative affairs of those new states of the area, Azerbaijan, Georgia and Armenia. This was easier said than done. Both Generals decided that, in order to ensure the safety of their own troops, they could not ignore the total chaos which was ensuing in the area. Thomson proclaimed Martial Law and became Military Governor of Baku. British Military Police maintained order, the British ran the banks, they brought in food rationing, they set up a labour control office and they returned to private ownership the oil and shipping industries which had been nationalized. There can rarely have been such a deliberate and flagrant flouting of direct orders to the contrary. However, the Foreign Office reported in a memorandum that it was necessary for the British to re-establish an administration in almost every department of the country's life.[4] An example of Thomson's proclamations appears at Appendix E.

British soldiers, however, were not free of Bolshevik propaganda. An example of an actual leaflet distributed in Baku is reprinted on page 113.

Tiflis, on the other hand, was not subjected to the same kind of alien administration. The Georgian authorities had not been superseded when the Germans arrived and their administration was relatively efficient.

Lieutenant Baker of the 1st Battalion Royal Scots arrived in Tiflis in early January 1919.[5] At first the Georgians were not at all friendly, seeing the British as very doubtful replacements for the Germans under whom order had been maintained and who had prevented their enemies, the Tsarist and Bolshevik Russians and the Moslem Azerbaijanis, from attacking or molesting them in other ways. However, as time went on and the Georgians saw that the British, like the Germans, were able to maintain order and protect them, the situation improved. Baker describes how they were welcomed into shops and restaurants and the opera, and how he was welcomed into Georgian homes. He went duck shooting. He then went to Baku where the situation was very difficult, with strikes and riots and much Bolshevik propaganda. However, on his return to Tiflis on 18 March 1919 he played polo and shot deer and boar – the latter activity being followed by a three-hour orgy of eating and drinking.

Similar events are recorded by A.S. Page, whose documents include the race card for the Tiflis Area Meeting on Wednesday 18 June 1919 which included the following events:

1. *Mules – for Indian NCOs and men over flat country – three furlongs*
2. *Horses – for British NCOs and men over flat country – three furlongs*
3. *Horses – open to officers Tiflis area – one mile. Seven jumps*
4. *Mules – for British NCOs and men – four furlongs*
5. *Horses – for officers Tiflis area – four furlongs*
6. *Horses – open to Georgian, Armenian and Russian civil and military population – approximately one mile – six or seven jumps*
7. *Horses – for officers of the Tiflis area over flat country – four furlongs*

8.   *Mules – for British NCOs and men – seven jumps – one mile*
       [there is no record as to how well the mules jumped]
Rules included:
       No other ranks are allowed to ride in officers' events.
       Dress will be helmets and shirtsleeves (no spurs in events 1
       and 4. Spurs allowed in event 8).
       No bookmakers.[6]

It must have been an astonishing event.

Apart from the rather tiresome guard duties involved in guarding the twenty-four bridges and tunnels on the railway between Batum and Baku there were no great military problems to be faced by the British Army in Tiflis. There were some minor health problems, as was shown in an order[7] signed by Captain H. Martin, Staff Captain RA 27th Division, on 26 January 1919.

> *The water in Tiflis is extremely bad and more dangerous than in any other town in which units of the divisional artillery have yet been billeted, and on no account is it to be drunk in any form unless thoroughly boiled or chlorinated or preferably both. This is to be brought to the knowledge of all ranks and severe disciplinary action will be taken in all cases where this order is disobeyed. It is pointed out that it is quite useless to boil the water, unless it is kept at boiling point for at least twenty minutes. If the water is merely heated and then allowed to cool the process is quite useless.*[7]

The situation in Batum, however, was quite different. Major Beresford Ash describes how:

> *During the first six weeks of our occupation, our troops were busily engaged in rounding up and evacuating all the Turkish troops and other undesirables: the former gave little or no trouble; their men were utterly demoralised, half starved, miserably clad and had received no pay for months and were only too glad to march on board our transport in Batum and be conveyed back to Constantinople as soon as possible. The Germans, however, gave a considerable amount of trouble and it took some considerable time to round up and dispose of them.*[8]

133

Beresford Ash then describes the situation which arose when the British merchant marine crew refused to carry German soldiers in their ship back to Constantinople:

> *After the way the Boche submarines had sunk and drowned so many of their comrades during the war nothing would induce them to carry Germans on board their ship. They eventually agreed to take the German women and children, but they threatened to throw the German officers into the harbour if they did not leave their ship immediately. The German officers then left and were taken to Constantinople crowded together in a small boat.*

The political and ethnic situation in Batum after the British arrival was extremely confused. The town had been under Tsarist rule for a century or more until the revolution but the Germans had taken it, the Turks had coveted it, the Georgians claimed it, the Bolsheviks were determined to grab it and, as we shall see later, General Denikin's anti-Bolshevik Volunteer Army, while it was being victorious, attempted to annex it. On top of all that there were thousands of refugees from the north attempting to escape what they saw, with some justification, as the murderous Bolshevik hordes.

During the Spring of 1919 Denikin appointed his own representative, General Romanovski, as Military Governor of Batum. This turned out to be a futile gesture and he was totally unable to control events. Food supplies ran out, hunger riots occurred, there was much looting and the British had to intervene. The British Military Governor made a coup d'etat, abolished the existing Council and installed his own British military officers in their place. The old legal code was re-installed and Beresford Ash explains:

> *A Major of twenty years' experience on the Stock Exchange in civil life, combined the duties of Prime Minister and Chancellor of the Exchequer; another officer who normally was land agent to a large estate in the south of England, became Home Secretary and Mayor of Batum town; the law courts were put under the control of a legal expert, who had spent many years on the West*

Coast of Africa as a Magistrate in the Colonial Civil Service; and other officers whose professions in civil life gave them the necessary experience were placed in charge of the customs posts and telegraphs and other public departments. Certain officers, too, were placed on a food council, to introduce a regular flow of supplies and to supervise food rationing, which was at once instituted . . . the appalling difficulty of the language question was overcome by the appointment of numerous interpreters in each department. Decisions on all local matters were made by the officer in charge, subject to the approval of the Military Governor.

Beresford Ash goes on to say:

Such was the form of government created by the British which lasted during the whole of the occupation until our final evacuation which took place in June 1920 and which was functioning in Batum when I arrived there on 2 June 1919.

On arrival, Beresford Ash found himself acting as Labour Minister, trying to settle strikes. He had to deal with delegates from 'the Union of Unions, a noisy collection of demagogues which had come into being as a result of the revolution'.

It was not long before a food crisis developed and Beresford Ash was sent to Constantinople to attempt to get shipments of food. He was then put in charge of passports and had to deal with the myriad problems of that job in that situation.

The great problem at that stage for the now-dwindling British force in Batum was that of uncertainty. What were they to say when asked what the British intentions were? The only answer they could give, truthfully, was, 'We do not know', and that was not very satisfactory when the whole future of the questioner and what he should do about it depended on the answer. Arguments one way or another in the Eastern Committee in London and in the Supreme War Council were one thing. The results on the ground were another. It must have been a matter of the utmost frustration to those in charge in Batum.

Of all the functions which British Army officers had been asked to undertake, the formation of a complete government,

Prime Minister, Home Secretary, etc, etc, at an area to the east of the Black Sea of which, probably, few of those taking part had previously heard, must be one of the strangest. It says a lot for their poise, intelligence and fair-mindedness that they managed it at all, although an English journalist C.E. Bechhofer found that the interpreters,

> a collection of Levantines and Jews, with a sprinkling of Russian ex-officers, were very open to corruption. . . . But, when nobody knew, least of all the British, how long we were to remain in Batum, or to whom, supposing we went away, the Province would be entrusted, how could one expect the local population to co-operate in exposing and clearing away the abuses of the administration?[9]

He paints a jaundiced view of so-called society at the time:

> In any restaurant in Batum you could see ladies of good family and education waiting on speculators and their prostitute companions while outside in the rain a Russian officer, too badly wounded, too demoralized or too much bound by family ties to be able to join Denikin's army could be seen carrying a portmanteau of a fat Odessa merchant.

The transition from British to Bolshevist rule in Baku in July 1919 was far from being a clear cut affair. Seaman Gunner Stan Smith found himself as a volunteer taking equipment for repairing guns and engines from Batum to Baku by train.[10] The train got stuck in the foothills of the Caucasian Mountains. They retrod their steps to Batum and, with all their stores, moved by boat and train through the Caspian to Persia, to Baghdad and thence to Enzeli, whence they found their way to Baku. However, the Bolsheviks entered the town. 'I was working quietly away when "bang". I knew no more. I had been fairly effectively bashed over the head and when I woke up I was trussed up like a chicken with both hands behind my back and my feet lashed tightly together.' With his friends he was cast into prison. His first meal was more like dish water and half a round of black bread. This was a picnic compared with the reality to come.

136

Immediately after that skimpy meal we were marched into the courtyard and given ringside seats or standing positions to watch the first massacre. There were about forty prisoners to be killed, men and women, and their captors used every atrocity imaginable.

One by one they slit the women up the middle to about the chest bone, disembowelled them and left them standing until they'd done the whole crowd of women. Then they shot them as they lay moaning and screaming on the ground. They made some of the men dip their arms into buckets of acid which was so strong that when they removed their arms the flesh hung down like huge gauntlets. We were forced to watch all this, helpless to do anything about it . . . we had to witness many more of these massacres before we were freed. Each time we were marched back to our cell to a life which grew more grim and we were perpetually hungry.

Smith was kept in prison for almost a year. The Georgians were still holding out against the Bolsheviks, but they managed to get agreement to move the prisoners to Tiflis, whence they went to Batum and home.

Such was the result of the British occupation of the Caucasus for one sailor and his companions. Their leader, who maintained his courage and dignity throughout the ordeal, was Commander Bruce Fraser, later Admiral Sir Bruce Fraser, who commanded the Home Fleet at the time of the sinking of the *Scharnhorst* in the Second World War.

The final British troops left Batum in June 1920. The evacuation was described in a letter by G. Le Brun, a sailor on the British ship *Field Marshal*, an ex-German ship which had been captured at Dar es Salaam:

There were three republics. Batum was in Georgia. The rich, which were driven from their homes by the Bolsheviks, made for Batum as it was safe, as they thought. There were duchesses, princesses, society girls and women working in restaurants and bar parlours. One of our stokers came aboard with a beautiful woman he claimed was a princess and she looked it. Many of the women wanted to marry us as they had heard that Georgia was to be turned over to the Bolsheviks . . . we were the last ship to leave after the Bolsheviks moved in. When the Union Jack was lowered the Durham Light Infantry played God Save the King, then up went the Hammer and Sickle. Our General and the Bolshevik Commander shook hands . . . our trip from Batum to Constantinople was a scene never to be forgotten or will ever be seen again. As we were moving from the dock the Durham's band was on the boat deck playing Auld Lang Syne. Women were jumping into the water. Some tried to climb aboard, others were trying to drown. But I think Admiral Seymour guessed what was happening. There were many picket boats from the warships and they fished the women out and took them back ashore . . .' Le Brun goes on, with glorious banality, 'It was nice in Batum as there were palm trees.'[11]

Chapter Seven

SOUTH RUSSIA

As we have seen, the main Allied aim after the first and, indeed, the second Russian Revolution was to find some way of keeping Russia in the war against Germany, thereby averting the whole-sale transfer of the German forces in the Eastern to the Western Front. Sir George Buchanan, the British Ambassador and, later, Bruce Lockhart, the unofficial link between the British and Soviet Governments, worked hard to avoid the disaster of a separate peace. The mass of the Russian Army and, indeed of the nation as a whole, however, were only too glad to make peace almost at any price to bring an end to the horrors they had been experiencing. In retrospect, it is clear that there never was the slightest chance of keeping Russia fighting. But there were some generals in the Russian Army who still perceived it as their duty to continue the war and, hopefully, to recreate greater Russia as it was. A number escaped from the chaos around Moscow and St Petersburg, arrived in the south and started to assemble armies, mainly, although not entirely, composed of officers dedicated to continuing the war against Germany and defeating the Bolsheviks. In addition to these elements, in the south there were the Cossacks, fiercely independent, tough but unpredictable, who never accepted the new situation brought about by the Revolution and, as in Siberia, a number of local swashbuckling bandits whose adherents were mainly interested in loot and the other perquisites of war.

General Alekseev, who had been Chief of Staff of the Imperial Army and General Kornilov, who had vainly attempted to seize Moscow during the later stages of the Kerensky regime, both arrived in the south in December 1917. A so-called 'Volunteer Army' was set up with its headquarters at Novocherkassk. At first it was viewed with great suspicion by the Don Cossacks under the Ataman (elected leader) Kaledin who wanted to be left alone to manage their own affairs and were worried that the Volunteer Army would antagonize the local Bolsheviks – which of course they did. Furthermore, Kornilov and Alekseev were at odds, the former a man of action, the latter a strategist and staff officer. Eventually, however, they came to an agreement, drafted by Alekseev's Chief of Staff, General Denikin, to the effect that Alekseev should have control over finance, civil government and relations with the Allies, Kornilov should act as Commander in Chief of the Army and Kaledin should retain responsibility for the administration of the Don Cossacks and for the Don Cossack force.

On 9 January 1918 Kornilov and Alekseev issued a joint statement in which they summed up their 'common policy':

> *The first aim of the Volunteer Army is to resist an armed invasion of South and South East Russia . . . It will defend to the last drop of its blood the autonomy of the territories which give it sanctuary and which are the last bastion of Russian independence, the last hope for the restoration of a true, Great Russia. But, together with this, the Volunteer Army has also other aims . . . [It] will stand guard over civil liberties until the day comes when the master of the Russian land, the Russian people, can express its will through the election of a Constituent Assembly.*[1]

Against the advice of Sir George Buchanan and General Knox, the vastly knowledgeable and influential Military Attaché at St Petersburg, the British Government decided that 'All national groups who are determined to continue the war must be supported by all the means in our power'.[2]

The Treaty of Brest Litovsk was ratified by a Special Congress of Soviets on 15 March 1918. The Germans began to move into the Ukraine and to set up a puppet government at Kiev. They assumed responsibility for most of the Ukraine and, more or less, maintained law and order until the Armistice of 11 November.

The Germans then began to leave and the Bolsheviks started to invade from the north. In these circumstances, in accordance with the secret agreement with Britain mentioned on page 101, the French landed in Odessa. Some 1,800 infantry arrived on 18 December 1918 to be joined, rather surprisingly, by two Greek divisions and some Rumanians, together with a brigade of Polish volunteers, followed, later, by other French troops, including many Senegalese and Algerian units – a total of some 80,000 men. They occupied the whole of the Black Sea coast from Rumania to the Crimea.

This was a marked contrast to the British policy of support for the White forces in the south which, as we shall see, was in theory confined to military supplies and instructors.

The French foray into the Ukraine did not last long. After the prolonged agonies of the war, French soldiers were not inclined to risk their lives in a totally confused situation in which it was difficult to understand any French interest. The apparent intention of the French intervention, to unite all anti-Bolshevik factions into a common cause, turned out to be a totally impossible task. A three-cornered battle was raging between Ukrainian nationalist forces, the Volunteer Army and the Bolsheviks. In addition, there were partisan bands led by a Cossack adventurer, Ataman Grigorev. The French, Greek, Polish, White Russian and Rumanian defenders of Odessa vastly outnumbered their attackers, but their morale was non-existent. They all evacuated Odessa on 6 April 1919 and the town fell, first to Grigorev and then to the Bolsheviks. As was to be the case elsewhere, the evacuation was swiftly followed by mass executions. Similarly, at Kherson, a port to the east of Odessa, the Greeks, who had fought bravely against Grigorev's partisans, apparently committed an appalling massacre of some 500 men, women and children as they retreated. As a reprisal, when his troops eventually captured the town, Grigorev ordered that every Greek prisoner of war should be shot.[3]

The only British entanglement in these affairs at that stage consisted of the navy, which helped the French who also supervised the evacuation of the Germans from Sevastopol. The French attitude to any further entanglement in Russian affairs

141

became very clear when, a fortnight later, the French Black Sea Navy was torn by a major mutiny.

Further east the White situation gradually became clear. Ataman Kaledin committed suicide after a temporary defeat and was succeeded by Ataman Krasnov in command of the Don Cossacks. General Kornilov was killed in action and General Alexeev died. General Denikin assumed command of the Volunteer Army and Krasnov agreed, reluctantly, to come under his overall command. Denikin began to win victories over the Bolsheviks and to advance north. He also found himself fighting with the Ukrainian nationalist leader Petlura, who refused to accept that Ukraine should remain part of Greater Russia. He had great problems in administering the territories which he had captured. Nevertheless, the British began to provide massive support without actually providing any fighting soldiers. The British Military Mission reached Denikin's headquarters at Ekaterinodar on 26 November 1918.

The reasons for the British decision to continue to intervene in Russia after the Armistice with Germany were set out by Lord Milner, the Secretary of State for War, in an open letter released to the press on 18 December 1918. He wrote that intervention had originally taken place to rescue the Czech Corps in Siberia and 'to prevent those vast portions of Russia which were struggling to escape the tyranny of the Bolshevists from being overrun by them and so thrown open as a source of supply to the enemy.' He continued, 'In the course of this Allied inter-vention thousands of Russians have taken up arms and fought on the side of the Allies. How can we, simply because our own immediate purposes have been served, come away and leave them to the tender mercies of their and our enemies, before they have had time to arm, train, and organize so as to be strong enough to defend themselves? It would be an abominable betrayal, contrary to every British instinct of honour and humanity.'[4]

The scale of the provision of military supplies to Denikin's forces was massive. Major-General Holman, who commanded the British Military Mission in South Russia, stated in his final report that between March 1919 and March 1920 Denikin's

142

forces were supplied with more than 1,200 guns and nearly 2 million shells, 6,100 machine guns, 200,000 rifles, 500 million rounds of small arms ammunition, more than half a million complete uniforms, 629 trucks and ambulances, 279 motor-cycles, seventy-four tanks, six armoured cars, 100 aircraft, twelve 500-bed general hospitals, twenty-five field hospitals, and large amounts of communications and engineering equipment. Nearly all came from the vast dumps which had grown up during the war at Salonika and other ports on the Mediterranean. With the exception of the aircraft, little was shipped from Great Britain.[5]

This material nearly all came through the Black Sea port of Novorossisk.

As was the case in Siberia the corruption and sheer inefficiency was appalling. Much of the military material rotted on the quays. As Commander Bostok put it in a letter to his mother, 'Clothing was all taken by the staff or sold. The front line got nothing'.[6] John Ernest Hodgson, a journalist with Denikin's armies, wrote in a book in 1922 that among the British hospital supplies were 1,500 nurses' uniforms. He never saw one on a Russian nurse but he saw 'girls who were emphatically not nurses walking the streets of Novorossisk wearing regulation British hospital skirts and stockings. During the battle in which the Red Army captured Kharkov in November 1919, British anti-freeze fluid was sold across the bar of the Hotel Metropole to be drunk while lorries and tanks froze for the lack of it.'[7]

Lieutenant Farmer noted in his diary that when he was Railway Transport Officer at Taganrog, at the time Denikin's Headquarters, 'There was tremendous corruption and theft from our supply wagons. The theft, pillage and almost open corruption became so serious that the British recruited Bolshevik prisoners, dressed them, armed them in full British kit, gave them full army rations and Private's Bag (sic) and formed a corps of guards over supplies. I had two men under me and we steadily reduced the loss of supplies so that the men were completely faithful to Britain.'[8]

A further problem as far as the British support for Denikin was concerned was the vicious anti-Semitism of the White Army.

There was a belief, probably because of the fact that Trotsky and other Bolshevik leaders were Jewish, that Bolshevism was a Jewish plot and that all Jews were Bolshevists. This was, of course, totally untrue, but there were undoubtedly many pogroms and other atrocities committed by White troops. Churchill became extremely worried about this situation and on 9 October 1919 telegraphed to Denikin urging him 'to redouble efforts to restrain anti-Semitic feeling and to vindicate the honour of a Volunteer Army'.[9] Denikin did make some concessions but anti-Semitic outrages continued.

Although they were not supposed to become involved in the fighting, some 'instructors' from the British Mission certainly did.[10] The British had given the White Russians some RE8 aircraft and part of the British Mission to Denikin's army consisted of flying instructors. The RE8s were far from up-to-date and had many faults. Nevertheless, the British set up a training wing and many White Russian pilots were given elementary instruction, which in fact consisted of only about four hours dual flying. Then, apparently without any excuse at all, a whole squadron of forty-seven aircraft was sent from Salonika to help Denikin's army. This consisted of DH9s for reconnaissance and bombing and Sopwith Camels to protect them. The squadron landed at Novorossisk on 18 June 1919. It was immediately engaged in action in the area of the town of Tsaritsyn (later Stalingrad) on the Volga which, as in the Second World War, was in a highly strategic position. A number of bombing and strafing missions were carried out, the aircraft being particularly successful in attacking the Bolshevik cavalry. However, the heroic exploits of this squadron could not be kept secret indefinitely and heavy criticisms began to be heard in London. A further façade was hastily erected, the squadron changing its name to 'A Squadron' and all its personnel, officers and men, being required to sign a form explicitly volunteering for service in South Russia, although some refused and were sent home.

To begin with, Denikin's army had great successes. It recaptured Odessa and advanced north through Kharkov, Kursk and Orel to within 250 miles or so of Moscow. The commander of the RAF Training Mission based at Taganrog, Lieutenant

Colonel Maund, saw an opportunity for his men to see some action themselves and sent some of his instructors up the line, with their aircraft, under the designation of 'Z' flight. They were given a train upon which were loaded six RE8 aircraft and they steamed north, stopping every now and again to unload the aircraft, undertake some flying mission, rejoining the train and moving north again. It was on one such occasion that they worked out that they were far enough north in order to bomb Moscow and asked for permission to do so. However, Churchill had foreseen this possibility and, aware of the adverse publicity which would result from this exploit and realizing that it would have no military value, he had already told Holman that any request of this nature should be refused.

As well as this, the British sent what was known as the South Russia Tank Detachment. This originally consisted of ten officers and fifty-five other ranks together with six Mark 5 and six Medium A tanks, the latter known as Whippets. They landed at Batum on 13 April 1919 and went to Ekaterinodar, Denikin's headquarters at the time, and started to train Russians to man the tanks. In fact the British instructors quickly became involved in the fighting and on 19 June a tank manned by British soldiers led a successful White Russian attack on Tsaritsyn. In July 1919 more tanks and instructors arrived, bringing the eventual total to fifty-seven Mark 5s and seventeen Whippets. The British instructors found the Russians very adaptable and easy to train and, in spite of the eventual White Russian defeat, the tanks were extremely useful to the White Russians, the Reds becoming greatly in awe of these strange and, to them, entirely new monsters.

The War Office Establishment Table of the South Russian Tank Detachment included the following:

	Boxing gloves	Sets	4
Footballs	Association		6
	Bladders		12
	Rugby		6
	Bladders		12

Writing in the Tank Corps Journal of March 1922, Sergeant Windle said, 'Took six Mark 5s and six Whippets to South Russia . . . Went to Ekaterinodar . . . We played a game of football against the Russians. They must have thought it was a free fight or wrestling match: they were new to the game. We lost by two goals to one and I thought we were lucky to get away with a whole skin.'

Denikin's forces had captured Orel, the furthest north they managed to reach, on 13 October 1919 – but they were quickly ousted from there by the Red Army and began a precipitate retreat.

As with Kolchak's advance earlier, the appearance was there, but not the reality. Churchill covers this in matchless prose in his book *The Aftermath*:

During the year 1919 there was fought over the whole of Russia a strange war; a war in areas so vast that considerable armies, armies indeed of hundreds of thousands of men, were lost – dispersed, melted, evaporated; a war in which there were no real battles, only raids and affrays and massacres, as a result of which countries as large as England or France changed hands to and fro; a war of flags on the map, of picket lines, of cavalry screens advancing or receding by hundreds of miles without solid cause or durable consequence; a war with little valour and no mercy. Whoever could advance found it easy to continue; whoever was forced to retire found it difficult to stop. On paper it looked like the Great War on the Western and Eastern fronts. In fact it was only its ghost; a thin, cold, insubstantial conflict in the Realms of Dis. Koltchak first and then Denikin advanced in what were called offensives over enormous territories. As they advanced they spread their lines ever wider and ever thinner. It seemed that they would go on till they had scarcely one man to the mile. When the moment came the Bolsheviks lying in the centre, equally feeble but at any rate tending willy-nilly constantly towards compression gave a prick or a punch at this point or that. Thereupon the balloon burst and all the flags moved back and the cities changed hands and found it convenient to change opinions, and horrible vengeances were wrecked on helpless people, vengeances perseveringly paid over months of fine-spun inquisition. Mighty natural or strategic barriers, like the line of the Volga River or the line of the Ural Mountains, were found to be no resting places; no strategic consequences followed from their loss or gain. A war of few casualties and unnumbered executions! The tragedy of each Russian city, of loyal families, of countless humble households might fill libraries of dreary volumes.[11]

He goes on to describe the reactions of the peasants to these events:

There they were and there they stayed; and with hard toil, there they gained their daily bread. One morning arrives a Cossack patrol. "Christ is risen; the Allies are advancing; Russia is saved; you are free. The Soviet is no more." And the peasants grunted, and duly elected their Council of Elders, and the Cossack patrol rode off, taking with it what it might require up to the limit of what it could carry. On an afternoon a few weeks later, or it may be a few days later, arrived a Bolshevik in a battered motor car with half a dozen gunmen, also saying, "You are free; your chains are broken; Christ is a fraud; religion is the opiate of democracy; Brothers, Comrades, rejoice for the great days that have dawned." And the peasants grunted. And the Bolshevik said, "Away with the Council of Elders, exploiters of the poor, the base tools of reaction. Elect in their place your village Soviet, henceforward the sickle and hammer of your Proletarian rights." So the peasants swept away the Council of Elders and re-elected with rude ceremony the village Soviet. But they chose exactly the same people who had hitherto formed the Council of Elders and the land also remained in their possession. And presently the Bolshevik and his gunmen got their motor car to start and throbbed off into the distance, or perhaps into the Cossack patrol.[12]

The British involvement was not only concerned with the supply of materials, training and some unofficial fighting. Captain Lancaster RA was sent to Odessa as Intelligence Officer to the British Military Mission there. In his diary for 24 November 1919 he states, 'Saw a censor and got him to jump on the *Contemporary Word* (a Russian language newspaper) for printing notices of the British intention to recruit Jews.'[13] On the same day he opened a British Reading Room and censored the English papers. He had clearly been anticipating orders to that effect because on 25 November he notes, 'Kursk lost to the Reds. Received orders from Major Owen (his boss) to act as British censor of all British papers placed in the Reading Room. Also on all British radio telegrams arriving.' The British authorities were clearly worried about the effect on the morale, both of their own soldiers and of the White Russians, of reading about the criticisms of intervention being voiced in the British press. One wonders what the effect would have been in Britain if it had become known that British troops serving in Russia had not been allowed to read their own national press.

However, the authorities were not able to cover up speeches made by Lloyd George in the House of Commons where he not only made it clear that in the last resort Britain would abandon the Volunteers, but on 17 November 1919 he cast considerable doubt about Denikin's aim of fighting for a reunited Russia, 'It is not for me to say whether that is a policy which suits the British Empire.'[14]

These speeches were widely disseminated and, undoubtedly, served to undermine still further the morale of the Volunteer Army.

Things went from bad to worse as the scale of Denikin's rout intensified. Evacuations began both from Odessa and Novorossisk.

A flavour of the situation as it had been in the Odessa area is given by a somewhat vainglorious letter written from Scotland by Major McPherson on 6 July 1920 to an American friend;

My dear Dyson . . . in France on 28 September 1918 I got piped in the shoulder and pretty badly gassed – couldn't settle down and volunteered for South Russia. I was sent out as Vickers machine gun instructor to the anti-Bolshevik forces then operating around Odessa. I had a very good time with the Russkies for about five months. I met a lot of the American Red Cross in Odessa and had a very good time with them. I was getting on like a house on fire when the crash came. I visited practically every regiment in Denikin's army and had a good time in Rostov, Taganrog, Kharkov, Novgorod and Kiev. I settled down in Odessa in October 1919 . . . I opened a machine-gun school of instructors for the Vickers. We were supplying Denikin with about 3,000

Vickers per month and the Russkies knew nothing about them. I tried the best with their reorganization but it was a pretty hopeless task owing to the carelessness of the Russian company commanders. I started instructing about the end of November and I had passed about 1,000 when the crash came on 7 February 1920. I was training 550 ex-Bolsheviks and 250 cadets . . . I was sent out of Odessa with my 800 men to dig a line from the Black Sea to the Rumanian border (thirty-five miles). They gave me forty-eight hours to do the job. What a hope! I was only six hours at work when I was rushed by about 500 Bolsheviks . . . Great sport but it only lasted about ten minutes. They were caught in the open with ten Vickers . . . this should never have happened as the Chief told me that the whole of the Tenth Corps was in front of me. I heard later that the whole of this Corps went over to the Bolshies. We started fighting at about 7 am on 6 February. We held our own. We had neither infantry nor heavy guns supporting us. I had about 150 Vickers average five men to a gun. At 10 am on 7th the 500 ex-Bolsheviks or what was left of them turned on me and the 250 cadets. I was in a rather nasty position as I was the only British officer on the spot. I was going along on horseback when a couple of the senior officers came up to me and told me to dismount. I could see from their ugly faces that their crowd had turned. I simply let one have the top of my boot and the other my whip and rode like the devil to that part of the line held by the cadets. They were boys aged from fourteen to nineteen but they stuck to me like the very devil. I started a rearguard action with all the Bolshies in the world trying to beat me up. I got to within five kilos of Odessa when one of my cadet officers was shot through the head. Like the D fool I was I decided to ride back. He was dead. It was while feeling his heart that the trouble started. A burst of MG fire riddled my own nag. I was in a right fix. Two kilos from the cadets and half a dozen of my former officers after me . . . they caught me through the leg and gave me six digs with the butt ends of their rifles, breaking five of my ribs. They threw me over a horse intending to take me back as a prize when they went over to the Bolshies. By good luck a crowd of cadet officers saw what was happening and saved me. I was taken back to Odessa, put on a battleship and taken to Constantinople, where I lay for six weeks absolutely unconscious. To top the bill I developed that awful typhus while in hospital . . . having been brought up in a hard school as a youngster, my constitution stood the strain.[15]

149

An equally personal, but perhaps more accurate, description of life in the British Mission appears in the journal written by Captain (later Major-General) Wood. As a subaltern in the 1st Dorsets he had been wounded in France and had not returned to his battalion when the armistice left him stranded. He volunteered to serve in Russia and, in early 1919, joined the British Mission at Ekaterinodar, Denikin's Headquarters. His first job was, with another young officer, to go forward to Novocherkassk to report on the activities of the Don Cossacks who, he was told, had recently changed sides and were fighting for Denikin's cause against the Bolsheviks. With the flimsiest knowledge of Russian gleaned from Hugo's First Russian Primer he found himself acting as interpreter.

> My first obvious duty was to print the name of our destination in Russian capitals for comparison with the railway name-boards as we progressed northwards. Then there was one final requirement from the Mission – surely soldier-servants were essential to our dignity as emissaries. We were allowed only one, a tough, cynical old private of the Royal Norfolks, hardly to qualify as a gentleman's gentleman. After much anxious study of Russian script I was at last able to announce our arrival, but that was the end of my success as interpreter. We were surrounded on the platform by an inquisitive crowd, obviously most impressed by the British private in full marching order, standing rigidly in the "at ease" position, but neither my French nor Hugo's Russian made any contact. We hoped for better things when a rough-looking character, all beard and sheepskins, thrust forward with "My Fader Scotch". We welcomed our compatriot with enthusiasm, but he had exhausted his vocabulary. In the meantime the crowd had been helpful, a cab was produced and we were deposited at the local hotel. Soon all our difficulties were swept away.
>
> The dea ex machina made a tempestuous entry trailing a cloud of floating veils. British governesses in foreign ports have a distinguished niche in literature, but we were soon convinced that for force of character our protectress was beyond compare. Behind her back we spoke of her as the "Bride of Lamermoor" (those veils) but we accepted her guidance in all our activities without question. We must call officially on all the leading personalities

of the Don capital; no difficulty as she has educated their wives and children, and then we must make some desirable social contacts, which meant tea parties. "The Bride" took care to instruct us minutely in Russian etiquette, and our only difficulty came from the nervous tension we felt under her watchful eye. Then she was emphatic that the British presence must also be seen by the general public, so every evening at the fashionable hour she paraded us in the town park, admitting that as we both stood well over six feet tall she considered her countrymen did her credit. But without feminine initiative the British presence was far better advertised by our third member. Hearing a commotion in the hotel courtyard one evening, we looked down to see our old soldier showing his pictures; snakes and dragons writhed on his legs and arms, a fox-hunt ran in full cry down his back, the British Navy sailed on his chest, with his regimental badge of Britannia very properly overall.

Novotcherkask was a complete miniature capital, having a cathedral, the Ataman's palace with its ceremonial sentries of the bodyguard, dignified public offices and an equestrian statue of their hero Yermak, the conqueror of Siberia, dominating the pretty little park. Nor do I forget our hotel; it was generally ramshackle but its breakfasts demanded all the stars of the Guide Michelin, every morning bringing a generous bowl of fresh black caviare. The British presence was soon recognized by a command to an official dinner at the Palace, a colourful affair with most interesting plate on display and champagne of Georgia. The great industrial city of Kharkov had only recently fallen to the Whites, and there we found an English couple who had lived quietly through revolution and counter-revolution, selling their indispensable tea from the London market, and they kindly took us into their home.

Now we really worked hard, both to set up an establishment to train Russian officers and NCOs as instructors and at the same time to hasten the flow of our machine guns, with their spares and ammunition, from the base port to the battalions at the Front. Fortunately British warrant officers and NCOs were now coming out to the Mission, splendid men who were to set a fine example, and we secured a little cadre of infantry sergeants. No language difficulties ever prevented a British sergeant from imparting instruction, but in this field we made an amusing experiment. The British technical names for the innumerable parts of our

complicated weapons were untranslatable, so we gave each a
Russian name, as crude and ribald as possible . . .

During the spring and summer of 1919 South Russia was a
most cheerful place. The German occupation of the wheat-
growing belt under their Peace Treaty had restrained violence and
subsequently the Bolsheviks had taken power without the first
fury of Revolution which had spilled so much blood in Moscow
and the north. Bereavement was universal, but almost entirely by
honourable death for Holy Russia in the German war. Now every
soul was living in a glow of optimism; the Allies had arrived, first
the British in the North, and now the French, near at hand at
Odessa; Kolchak's army, with British support, had swept across
Siberia and was now on the Urals, and lately had come news of a
rising in Estonia, directly threatening St Petersburg itself. Soon
there must be victory, peace and the return home to re-build life
again.

Wood goes on to describe the success and then the collapse of
the White armies:

Ex-Sergeant-Major Budenny, in addition to his magnificent
moustache, had all the professional qualities required, and now
that the moment of decision had come, the nucleus of the mighty
Red Army was in existence. The victories of Denikin's army had
all been won by its spearhead, the Volunteer Division. Raised by
the revered General Kornilov, who had fallen at its head, this
formidable Division was a strange mixture of officers serving in
the ranks, young cadets from the Military Colleges and loyal
NCOs of the old army. Inspired by pure patriotism, military
tradition or revenge, all ranks wanted to fight and were prepared
to die. The last city to fall to us was Kursk, later to be so desper-
ately defended in the great tank battles of 1943, thence the
advance drove on to the outskirts of Orel and there Budenny met
the Volunteer Division head on and broke it.'

Wood was at first, as were very many people, clearly taken in by
the appearance of success: the reality was different.

At the news of the disaster to our formidable spearhead the whole
Front collapsed like a house of cards; complete battalions dis-

appeared, while desertion was reducing to mere skeletons those still held together by good officers. Then everywhere the stars in their courses turned against us.[16]

The attitude of many British servicemen was summed up by Captain Wyld RN, who went to Kherson near Odessa in command of the destroyer *Nereide*. He wrote in his diary:

Why don't we declare a policy of sorts? We haven't one and it is extremely difficult for all of us here to try to do what we can with nothing at our backs. People ask, "What are the Allies doing? When are the troops coming?" One isn't allowed to give an answer because there isn't one. The Germans came and took charge and did something and kept order. The Allies came and do nothing. If you can't do something, if you don't intend to do anything. We don't want you.[17]

The evacuations at Odessa, Novorossisk and, later, the Crimea were heartbreaking and pathetic affairs. The British Navy did what it could to take with them as many refugees as possible – but clearly there were limits. Captain Swinley recorded in his journal the following:

At first the town of Odessa seemed fairly quiet, but a feeling of unrest prevailed in spite of the optimistic views of General Schilling who, as Commander of the District, was apparently ready to hold the town against the Red Army. It soon transpired, however, that the town was in a very bad state, small riots and shooting affairs were frequent and the Authorities were most lax in dealing with these disturbances, although it must be said to their credit that when they did make any arrests, capital punishment (sic) was a foregone conclusion . . . on Saturday 1 February 1920 it was apparent that evacuation would shortly become necessary as Schilling seemed to be weakening . . . the scenes on the quay were very pathetic. It was found necessary to have at least two officers and about fifteen armed men on every ship to prevent the gangway being rushed. Schilling had apparently thrown in his hand quite voluntarily. We were given a company of cadets – a most efficient police force.
On 7 February 1920 the Reds were getting nearer. We now

began to embark the cadets and in five minutes the whole jetty became a mash of panic-stricken humanity.

We were originally intended to remove about 500 cadets and families but about 1,300 arrived. The younger ones, average age thirteen, won everybody's admiration. They came on board smiling and cheerful, without the slightest sign of nerves, more than could be said about their elder brothers. The enemy were not regular Red troops but armed bands of brigands.[18]

The scene at Novorossisk was clearly equally harrowing. Durnford (later Vice-Admiral) had volunteered for the Mission. As he says in his journal, partly because of the 'bloodthirsty monsters' (the Bolsheviks) but mainly because of the excitement and the prospect of command on foreign service, he set off in late September 1919. His first sight of Russia was at Odessa. 'I retain the memory of the haggard figure of a woman, a semi-lifeless figure, recumbent on the steps of a church, a figure symptomatic of the misery which swept the land. There were grim photographs of atrocities by the Bolsheviks.'[19] He then went to Novorossisk. His ship embarked 1,900 refugees. It was very cold and many died. The Green Guards, bandits, were around Novorossisk. Dawn brought with it the sound of artillery fire. His ship was filled to capacity and all craft inside the harbour made for the open sea, leaving behind the scenes of panic. The warships (British) opened fire on targets on the distant ridge. It was the death knell of the White Army and a prelude to the final collapse.

The final scene as far as the British were concerned was acted out at Sevastopol. Shrubsole (later Engineer Rear Admiral) describes the situation there in a letter from HMS *Calypso* to a Miss Jean Campbell:

The Crimea at present is the refuge of most of those loyalists and the aristocracy of Russia who have escaped the Bolsheviks . . . a host of Grand Dukes, Counts, Barons and other notorieties including the Grand Duke who killed Rasputin. The Bolsheviks are attacking the narrow land which joins the Crimea to the main-land and the French, Greeks and ourselves are helping the Volunteer Army defending the Crimea. As soon as the Crimea falls we shall evacuate all British subjects and the Russian nobility. The latter will be certain to be killed in a very cruel way if they were left but what worries us is the beastliness of leaving a host of other people of less exalted rank to the cruel fate which awaits them.[20]

In a later letter to the same person he says:

The French had about 4,000 troops ashore and the Greeks 2,000 but they were never sent to the fighting line. We could not understand the apathy of the French Admiral who was in command of the Allied forces. The Greeks wanted to assist more actively but were never allowed to. Finally, the Bolsheviks forced the lines, the Volunteer Army melted away and in a very short time the Crimea was overrun and the Allied forces besieged in Sevastopol. With orders from the French we started evacuating as many decent people as possible from the coast towns and removed 1,000 or more including the old Dowager Empress, Grand Duke Nicholas and a host of other notables. At Sevastopol things became very difficult. There were three French battleships, one Greek and our ship and some of our destroyers. The Bolsheviks started an attack one night and a proper battle took place, all the ships firing from the harbour and the troops ashore and the Bolsheviks firing as hard as they could. The Bolsheviks got jolly well smashed and eventually proposed an armistice which was agreed to for ten days . . . the crews of the French ships began to get disaffected. They were mostly hostility ratings [ratings taken on 'for hostilities only'] and wanted to get back to France. Things came to a head when all leave had to be stopped on account of the approach of the Bolsheviks. Finally, the day after the Bolsheviks had been repulsed the crews fell in and demanded leave. The French Admiral thought it better to give way and they went ashore. Ashore they met Bolshevik sympathisers and after being well filled with drink they started parading the town with a red flag at the head and eventually came in contact with the military and were fired upon by the Greek and French troops. They went on board again, hoisted the red flag on French ships at the jackstaff and refused all duty except to take the ships back to France. The upshot was that the French cleared out, lock, stock and barrel and we took command.

Shrubsole then describes how Bolshevik aeroplanes came over and dropped propaganda, 'of which I enclose a copy. It has been read to the men to show them what fools the Bolsheviks believe them to be.' (An exact copy of the propaganda leaflet is at Appendix F. By contrast, a fulsome welcome from the White General is attached at Appendix G).

After his defeat and the evacuation of Novorossisk Denikin resigned his command of the Volunteer Army. His most successful, and highly charismatic, Commander, General Wrangel, took his place. In April 1920 Denikin left for Constantinople in a British destroyer. Wrangel reorganized the Volunteer Army and the civil administration of the Crimea and even mounted a successful attack against the Bolsheviks. This was against British advice and the British Government decided on 11 November 1920 not to give Wrangel assistance in evacuating women and children, much less a fighting force. The French, however, had reacted to his offensive by recognizing him and offering him assistance in return for getting possession of all his ships to defray their expenses. In fact no fewer than 146,000 Russians elected to leave Russia in the final exodus, mostly in Wrangel's own ships, of which the French then took possession. The French did, however, help the refugees temporarily to settle in teeming camps around Constantinople.[21]

Thus, in ignominy, ended the Allied intervention in South Russia.

Chapter Eight

THE BALTIC

Compared to all the other Allied interventions in Russia in 1918/19 that in the Baltic was very minor and of no great importance in the general order of things. There were, however, two significant aspects to it. First, although the French did send a mission, a cruiser and two destroyers to the area, the action was almost entirely British, both in terms of the military effort involved and of those who took the decisions to intervene. Second, the political complications involved in the Baltic scene as the war ended were of a mind-boggling complexity to a greater degree than any of the other, also very complicated, situations that confronted those who attempted to understand and deal with events on the periphery of Russia.

For example, in his masterly and definitive work *The Baltic Revolution – Estonia, Latvia, Lithuania and the Path to Independence*, Anatol Lieven has the following paragraph:

In January 1919 after a Lithuanian rule of two months following the German collapse, Vilnius fell into the hands of the Bolsheviks. On 15 April it was captured by the Poles who later made it an autonomous region in the hope of using it to tempt Lithuania to restore the old confederation with Poland. At the time Vilnius was a mainly Polish/Jewish city with a Lithuanian minority variously estimated at between two and twenty percent. A year later, the Poles launched an offensive against Soviet Russia, were initially defeated, and handed Vilnius to the Lithuanians – after they had already lost it to the Bolsheviks. The Bolsheviks themselves gave it to the Lithuanians on 25 August in return for permission to cross Lithuanian territory on their way to attack the Poles. The

157

Poles then counter-attacked and defeated the Bolsheviks. At this time Poles and Lithuanians were also fighting each other, in a desultory way.'[1]

This kind of complexity was not confined to Lithuania: the Latvian and Estonian situations were equally obscure. So much so that the leader of the French Mission to Latvia, on appealing to his government for funds, was authorized to draw up to 1,000 yen, the official at the Quai d' Orsay explaining later that he imagined Latvia to be a Japanese island.[2]

The three Baltic countries had been part of Greater Russia until the First World War, when the German Army had overrun them. After the second Russian Revolution in October 1917 when Bolshevik Russia made peace with Germany at the Treaty of Brest-Litovsk (3 March 1918) all three Baltic territories were ceded to Germany. Under Article Twelve of the Armistice of 11 November 1918, the Germans were to leave a small garrison at Libau in southern Latvia, the only area in Latvia not in Bolshevik hands, in order to maintain order and to look after the liquidation of remaining German assets. All the other German troops in the Baltic countries were to withdraw whenever the Allies thought the moment suitable. A German General, von der Goltz, arrived in Libau on 1 February 1919 ostensibly to take command of the German garrison there, but he had different ideas, hoping to be able to redeem his country's defeat in the West by holding on to some, if not all, of Germany's previous conquests in the area.

There was a further complication in the existence in Latvia of the German Balts, the descendants of the German Teutonic Knights and their followers who had been in Latvia since the twelfth century. Indeed, much of Latvia had been divided into great estates owned by these German conquerors. They had been followed by Hanseatic merchants and industrialists who dominated all Latvian trade. They maintained an uneasy relationship over the centuries with the native Letts and their nominal masters, Tsarist Russia. The various factions, therefore, competing for control in 1918/19 consisted of the Bolsheviks, the White Russians, the German Balts together with the German

Army under von der Goltz, the Baltic peoples themselves, the Allies and the Poles, with a strong interest in Lithuania. The nationalists, mainly composed of the indigenous people themselves, hoped for independence but were at times prepared to settle for German help in order to defeat the Bolsheviks. The Allies, in general, although at times there was some dissension, supported the nationalists, seeing Estonia, Latvia and Lithuania as possible buffers between the West and the feared Bolshevik regime in Russia. In general, although as always not being of one mind on this or indeed any other matter, the Allies were not prepared to back this view with force except, as far as the British were concerned, by sea. As we have seen, there was also a very small French presence. The British intervention was confined to Latvia and Estonia, Lithuania in practice being left to its own devices as the Germans, the Bolsheviks, the Poles and the Lithuanians themselves jostled and fought each other for position in bewildering complexity.

In November 1918 the British sent a fleet to the Baltic in order to enforce a blockade on Bolshevik Russia and to contain the Bolshevik fleet at Kronstadt, the naval base close to Petrograd. There was originally some justification for this blockade on the grounds that there was a legitimate reason for the blockade of Germany and hence the Baltic ports through which it was just possible, although extremely unlikely, that Germany might receive supplies, until the Treaty of Versailles was ratified by the German Diet, but after ratification on 9 July 1919 even this somewhat flimsy excuse vanished. War against the Bolsheviks had not been declared and the British were clearly in breach of international law in these actions. The original naval force under command of Rear Admiral Alexander-Sinclair consisted of five cruisers, seven destroyers and seven minesweepers. The Baltic was liberally sown with mines and, during the episode, a number of British ships struck mines and were damaged or sunk. In January 1919 Alexander-Sinclair's force was relieved by a force of two cruisers and five destroyers under command of Admiral Cowan, which was joined by the French naval force mentioned above. In February Cowan's force was relieved by two cruisers and five destroyers under Captain Cameron, Cowan returning with two more cruisers and ten destroyers in April. Further substantial naval reinforcements arrived in May.

The game of Musical Chairs indulged in by the British Admiralty certainly did not inhibit forceful action by the navy on the spot. Indeed, the British fleet was used to bombard the northern coast of Estonia on numerous occasions in support of the Estonian, and later the North-Western, Armies which were fighting the Bolsheviks.

Signalman Hunter, who arrived in the Baltic on HMS *Wakeful* on 1 December 1918 describes in his diary[3] how his ship bombarded the Bolsheviks on the North Estonian coast on 13 and 23 December causing very heavy casualties. He explains that the British fleet was there to show the British flag since the Germans had told the Russians that they had won the war and the English had been wiped out. He goes on to describe the bestial behaviour of the Germans and Bolsheviks alike. 'The Hun treatment of the Russians is terrible. They treat them like dogs . . . the experiences of the Russians raises one's blood against them. These Germans are cowardly dogs and we realize how glad and grateful we should be that our mothers and sisters in England have escaped such degrading experiences.' He then talks of the Bolshevik torture of the Estonians, putting their eyes out and using Chinese tortures. They are credited with terrible crimes. 'On one occasion an Estonian family all sat round a table in their home with a good meal set before them. Only their hands had been nailed to the table and their feet to the floor so they were starved to death with food only a few inches off their mouths.' He also describes how they captured two Bolshevik destroyers – the *Spartak* and the *Arotroille* – for which he received £10 from the Naval Prize Fund, surely not much of a reward.

Before dealing with the attacks on Kronstadt in which the British navy sunk two Bolshevik battleships and a cruiser with very small loss to themselves, we should examine two even more extraordinary occurrences. In October 1918 some extreme reactionary White Russians had formed what was known as the 'Northern Corps' in Estonia with the purpose of re-establishing the old order in Russia. They had originally hoped for German

160

support but after the armistice this was clearly not possible and they agreed to come under the command of the Estonian Army. In April 1919 General Yudenitch, a Tsarist General, arrived and took command of this force. They pushed the Bolsheviks back and liberated nearly all Estonia from Bolshevik control. At the same time von der Goltz, with a collection of volunteers sent out from Germany together with the German Balts – a formation known as the 'Baltic Landswehr' – launched a successful offensive in Latvia against the Bolsheviks and captured Riga where his troops set up a 'reign of terror' in the Foreign Office's phrase, some 3,000 inhabitants of Riga being slaughtered.[4] However, on advancing further in northern Latvia von der Goltz's army was conclusively defeated by Latvian and Estonian troops.

The British sent out a military mission under General Sir Hubert Gough, who had commanded the British Fifth Army until the German offensive of March 1918. He was accompanied by Stephen Tallents, a Board of Trade official who had been responsible for food aid in the area. Gough's job was to supervise von der Goltz's withdrawal to Germany with his troops. Tallents had with him a Lieutenant Colonel, the Hon Harold Alexander, DSO, MC (later Field Marshal Lord Alexander), aged twenty-seven, who had been an outstanding commander in the war, even at one period being the acting commander of the Fourth Guards Brigade. He had found the prospect of peacetime soldiering, 'too dull for words' and, having no ties in England, he had looked round for something more interesting: hence his attachment to an ex-fellow Guards officer Stephen Tallents.

In the spring and summer of 1919 the situation in northern Latvia and Estonia became even more confused. Von der Goltz hoped to be able to consolidate his position in the area by ostensibly himself retiring from the scene and placing what he called 'the Army of Western Russia' which he had formed out of about 12,000 anti-Bolshevik Russian ex-prisoners of war and the 30,000 or so Germans already in the Baltic provinces under the command of a Georgian adventurer, Colonel Bermondt-Avalov. In fact, control of this force remained in von der Goltz's hands. The Baltic Landswehr, however, on General Gough's insistence, was put under the command of Harold Alexander who therefore found himself commanding the equivalent of a brigade almost entirely officered by his ex-enemy. He very quickly reorganized this force into three battalions – 1,200, 950 and 850 strong – and established himself in undisputed command, generating great affection and loyalty in his subordinates of all nationalities.[5] The Estonian Army was engaged in bitter hostilities against the Bolsheviks who had advanced into the country. General Yudenitch was attempting to organize an attack on Petrograd from northern Estonia and trying to get support from General Mannerheim, the Regent of Finland, and his Finnish army. He failed in this endeavour, partly because the so-called Supreme Ruler of Russia, the White Russian Admiral Kolchak, in Siberia, refused to give a guarantee of Finnish independence and the Finns, for their part, demanded a guarantee of Finnish independence together with some territorial concessions. An attempt was then made by General Gough and his deputy, Brigadier Marsh, to persuade the Estonian Army to support General Yudenitch. Marsh went so far, under Gough's orders, as to actually form, under duress, a so-called Russian North-Western Government which would guarantee Estonian independence and support the attack on Petrograd. This was done without any authority from the British Government. Indeed, on 20 August 1919, the British Cabinet repudiated the actions of Gough and Marsh, reprimanded them and recorded a demand for their recall. Gough did return to England and attempted to defend himself but, apparently, Marsh remained in the Baltic area.

On 7 October 1919 Bermondt-Avalov's army attacked Riga but were driven out by the Letts with the support of gunfire by the British fleet. By sheer force of personality Alexander managed to restrain his, mainly German, Landswehr from joining Bermondt-Avalov's attack. Alexander's final contribution to the eventual independence of the Baltic states, and in particular of Latvia, came in early 1920 when the Landswehr joined the Letts on their left and the Poles on their right to drive the Bolsheviks out of the whole of Latvia.

Meanwhile, in the summer of 1919, the British Baltic fleet, under Admiral Sir Walter Cowan, had been active. The Admiralty had tested and then constructed a number of what they called coastal motorboats (CMBs), whose chief advantage lay in their speed (over thirty-six knots) and their very shallow draught (2' 9"), the latter due to their hydroplane type of hull. After the Revolution, when the British Embassy and all the Consulates in Russia had been closed, the British still retained a major source of intelligence and information in Petrograd (Paul, later Sir Paul, Dukes). There was great difficulty in keeping in touch with him and the then Lieutenant Agar was sent with two CMBs to southern Finland with the intention of landing agents somewhere in the vicinity of Petrograd with that purpose. Agar found a small cove, Terrioki, very close to the Russian border where, with great secrecy, he established a base. The sea approach to Petrograd was guarded by the island of Kronstadt, to the north and south of which were a number of smaller forts. Because of minefields it was impossible to approach Petrograd to the south of the island of Kronstadt but the defences between the forts to the north of the island consisted of a series of sunken breakwaters. These obstacles were sunk to a depth of about 3'. There were also mines sunk to a depth of 6'. It should, in theory, therefore, be possible for the CMBs to pass over both obstacles when at speed with 2" or 3" to spare over the breakwaters. With great panache and courage, Agar succeeded in passing over these obstacles and landing, and subsequently collecting, agents near Petrograd, although there were a number of hiccups and some failures in this process, notably in the last attempt to pick up Dukes himself who, with his companion, had a narrow escape when the rowing boat in which they set out to meet Agar sank and they had to swim ashore.[6]

Agar heard that the sailors in one of the Russian fortresses at Krasnaya Gorka had mutinied and that the Bolshevik navy in Kronstadt was certainly about to attack it. This seemed an ideal moment for him to disrupt the Bolshevik plans by sinking one of their ships with the torpedoes carried by his CMBs. In spite of having no orders from anyone to that effect (indeed he had clear orders to the contrary), Agar decided to attack the Bolshevik navy with his two CMBs. On their first approach one of them hit an obstruction. Agar then decided to attack on his own. He did so the following night, and sank a Bolshevik cruiser (the *Oleg*), later being decorated with the Victoria Cross for his exploit.

Admiral Cowan, a forceful and charismatic character if ever there was one, quickly realized the possibility of using a larger flotilla of CMBs in a major attack on the Bolshevik fleet at Kronstadt.[7] A plan was devised which included a diversionary attack by aircraft on the fort of Kronstadt during the naval operation. An aircraft carrier (in the event HMS *Vindictive*) was requested. A base was established at Biorko on the Finnish mainland. On 18 August, under Admiral Cowan's orders, the attack took place. The CMBs were under the command of a Commander Dobson. There was close cooperation with the RAF, which kept the Bolshevik gunners in the fortress heavily engaged while the flotilla of CMBs approached.

Squadron Leader Brewerton describes in his diary how, having left the Firth of Forth for the Baltic on 2 July 1919 in HMS *Vindictive* he helped to create an airport in Finland at Koivisto.[8] He was given gold worth £10, a revolver and a meat bribe ticket (sic) in case of a forced landing. He made his first attack on Kronstadt on 30 July flying his Camel 2 strutter [sic] aircraft, dropping his bombs at 5,000'. There was 'a lot of AA but nowhere near us'. His aircraft was fitted with extra tanks so there was no observer. He was airborne for two hours fifty minutes. He bombed Kronstadt again on 5 and 18 August (the day of the successful naval foray against the Bolshevik fleet). He resumed the attack on 22 and 30 August and on 3 September when the AA fire had become far more effective and he had to attack at 14,000' to 15,000' 'for safety'. He continued to attack on 6 and 13 February. On 13 August the oil pressure in his aircraft 'went' and he had to land in water but was rescued by a Finnish motor boat.

During the actual attack, guided by Agar with his by now very experienced boat and crew, there was very little room in the harbour itself where the Bolshevik ships were moored and this added greatly to the difficulties faced by the CMBs since their torpedoes could only be fired when their ship was at top speed. In the event a submarine depot ship was sunk, one battleship badly damaged and one battleship sunk. Three of the seven

164

CMBs were destroyed, eight British sailors were killed and nine captured. In spite of these losses, therefore, the attack was a triumphant success. Two Victoria Crosses, six Distinguished Service Orders, eight Distinguished Service Crosses and fifteen Distinguished Service Medals were awarded. Agar made one final attempt to pick Dukes up from the Russian shore near Petrograd on 23 August. His boat, however, hit a breakwater and total disaster loomed for a time until a Russian fishing boat appeared on the scene and, at gunpoint, towed them to safety.[9]

Henry McCall, later Admiral, was serving in HMS *Westcott* in the Baltic fleet under Admiral Cowan's command. In his diary he summed up his view of this and other events in the Baltic as follows:

> *The whole show is so intensely interesting when one is on the spot. And it has been grand to have an Admiral like Walter Cowan who has the respect of all. Everything that the navy has contrived to do in these parts has been on his initiative. We never publicly declared war on the Bolshies and are not therefore entitled to attack them. All we have been supposed to do has been to see that the Bolshie ships do not make a nuisance of themselves. If they opened fire we could have fired back to protect ourselves. That, however, has been no policy for our Admiral. He goes into attack and apologizes afterwards. He has the Admiralty behind him of course. They strop him officially and pat him on the back privately. The miserable Government don't know what to do or make of it. If only the Government had the right view we could have got the Bolshie ships finished off in no time.[10]*

There are echoes here of military men bemoaning the caution of politicians in all countries and times. What is a simple matter to one is highly complex to the other. The two genres never have and never will fully understand each other. Their purposes are inevitably and eternally different in virtually all contexts. In fact, in this case, the surprising thing is not that there were political doubts but that the navy was allowed to do what it did with the support, whether overt or covert, of its political masters.

The British navy, therefore, established complete control in the Baltic from its arrival in November 1918 to November 1919 when it left due to the onset of ice. This was not achieved cheaply. No less than 238 British naval vessels were employed in the Baltic, including twenty-three cruisers and eighty-five destroyers, with the daily average of twenty-nine up to 30 June 1919 and thereafter of eighty-eight up to 31 December 1919. One hundred and twenty-eight British officers, seamen and airmen were killed, while seventeen vessels (including one light cruiser and two destroyers) and thirty-seven aircraft were lost – the ships mainly by hitting mines.[11] Apart from the damage it inflicted on the Bolshevik fleet already mentioned, it bombarded the Bolshevik army on many occasions and it shelled the German force operating under Bermondt-Avalov as a front for von der Goltz. All this was not achieved without difficulties of morale. In his memoirs Captain Waymouth describes how, in the autumn of 1919, a half flotilla was ordered to leave Scotland for the Baltic:

> But the red bug had been doing its work and at a stormy meeting at Port Edgar, where the Commodore D talked to the sailors, mutiny broke out and the sailors refused to sail. The half flotilla sailed eventually but it was an ugly experience . . . they were not going to fight someone else's war, especially against the worker's soviets. The old ideas, traditions and loyalties no longer held in the face of war-weariness and the new ideas of class loyalty which cut across service and national ties.

There were, however, some recompenses. Sub-Lieutenant Hampsheir who was with Agar in his CMB during his successful attack on the Bolshevik cruiser and who kept his nerve at a crucial moment when the torpedo cartridges fired prematurely and a new one had to be inserted, received a bounty of £768 4s. 1d for his part in the action and a further £5 'Prize Fund'.[13] Hampsheir received the DSC for his work but unfortunately suffered from prolonged shock.

In the event the three countries, Estonia, Latvia and Lithuania, were unable to secure enough military support in order to mount any kind of real attack on the Bolsheviks in Russia itself, let alone a guarantee of permanent independence from the White

Russians. They therefore settled for separate treaties with the Bolsheviks, who wished to concentrate their forces against Denikin in the south and offered them independence without any strings. Britain, notably in the person of Winston Churchill, tried hard to get Kolchak in Siberia and Denikin in the south to guarantee independence to the Baltic states, but they both refused. In spite of the fact that the three Baltic Governments had told the Soviet Government at the end of September that they were prepared to enter into preparatory peace talks and the fact that this was well known, General Yudenitch persisted in his plan to attack Petrograd with his North-Western Army which consisted of some 17,000 combatants.[14] With this force were six British tanks manned with British crews.[15] The attack started on 12 October 1919 with some support from the guns of the British Baltic Squadron. After some initial successes the attack began to falter. Yudenitch implored the Finns to help him, but they refused. By 25 November the North-Western Army had ceased to exist. Peace treaties were signed by the Soviet Government with Estonia on 2 February 1920, Lithuania on 12 July 1920, Latvia on 11 August 1920 and Finland on 14 October 1920.

The hope of the British Government that the Baltic countries would not make a peace with the Bolsheviks, thereby forcing them to retain a substantial portion of their army in the area instead of transporting them to the south to fight against Denikin were, in the event, vain. Soviet forces were transported and, as we shall see, both General Denikin's and Admiral Kolchak's armies were annihilated. Von der Goltz and his German forces had to withdraw but that was, probably, inevitable in the long run. Something positive, however, emerged – the independence of the three Baltic countries from both the Germans and the Russians, which was to last for twenty years until the peace of Europe was again shattered in 1939.

Although very minor in the scale of matters at that time, the three manifestations of British intentions were remarkable: first the British Navy's attack on Kronstadt and its other activities in the Baltic, then General Gough's and Brigadier Marsh's extraordinary construction of a North-Western Russian Government without any authorization from their political masters and, lastly, Harold Alexander's astonishing feat in successfully commanding a largely German brigade in Latvia so soon after the end of the war. In addition to these three developments there were of course the six British tanks and their crews fighting with General Yudenitch's North-Western force in its attempt to capture Petrograd.

Chapter Nine

CONCLUSION

'As an episode in history, the Intervention suggests nothing so much as a game organized at the end of a children's party. The small guests embark on it with enthusiasm, the small host is delighted, for a time the fun is fast and furious. But the shadows lengthen, mothers and nannies appear in French windows, one by one the players are summoned in out of the cold, warned that it is time to go home; the pleas of the disconsolate host are ignored, the game peters out. The party is over, the curtains are drawn. Night falls.'[1]

Thus, in vivid, although perhaps dated, imagery, Peter Fleming describes the ill-fated foray into Russian affairs by no less than sixteen countries in 1918/20.

The leaders of the participating nations did, indeed, embark on the intervention with some enthusiasm, believing, or at least hoping, that, in the north and east, they would be able to prevent the Germans from shifting their entire efforts to the Western Front and, in the south, that they could avoid a massive shift of oil, cotton and other vital commodities to the predatory Central Powers. On the defeat of Germany and Turkey, this objective changed to be replaced, in part, by crude anti-Bolshevism, but, when it became clear that their anti-Bolshevik Russian allies were far from looking like the eventual winners in a civil war, were divided in their aims and prey to massive corruption, what enthusiasm the interventionists had became very quickly eroded. The participants in the Intervention did, indeed, one by one, go home. And the lights did go out.

The Allied Intervention in the internal affairs of Russia came about almost in a fit of absence of mind. The obvious need to keep Russia involved in the war against Germany and then to support those elements in Russia who wished to continue the fight led eventually, after the German defeat, to the aim of toppling the Bolshevik regime. At no stage was a conscious decision taken to change the objective; it just happened as the momentum engendered by the intervention took over. It was impossible, too, to evacuate the forces at Archangel in the winter of 1918/19 because Archangel was icebound. What were the soldiers there to do? The local commander had to be given some orders, if only guidelines, and an explanation for why they were there had to be given to the troops on the ground.

Furthermore, the Allies had, willy-nilly, acquired obligations to those anti-Bolsheviks whom they had supported initially because they were prepared to continue the fight against Germany. The Allies could not just desert them, or so it was persuasively argued.

And, even more strange, the War Office sent two divisions to Transcaucasia without consulting the Foreign Office: the Cabinet Committee in question did not even consider what they should do until after they had arrived.

One of the great problems which beset the British and, certainly, the other Western Allies, was the great lack of accurate information as to what was happening in central Russia. The decision of the Western Powers not to recognize the Bolshevik regime and, therefore, not to establish Embassies in Petrograd and, later, Moscow, meant that information on which decisions were taken was at best haphazard and, at worst, plain wrong. It was true that the Secret Services had agents of one sort and another at work but they were themselves almost always involved in one or other of the various factions which sprang up all over Russia in an attempt to seize power. Their information was, therefore, generally far from objective – and the authenticity of it open to some doubt. Paul Dukes in Petrograd, was an exception, but his experience seems to have been limited to what was happening in that town alone.

On the other hand, Britain had a great deal of information

about what was happening on the periphery of the Russian state – in the Far East, in the Caucasus, Transcaspia, the Baltic regions and the far north – since we had official agents of one sort and another varying from the Embassy itself, at first in Vologda and then in Archangel, to Consuls, High Commissioners, Liaison Officers and so on, in all these areas.

However, in the central Bolshevik redoubt, which was never to be captured by the anti-Bolshevik forces, there was very little information to be had, certainly after Bruce Lockhart left in October 1918 and his reports were not believed by those of the Cabinet who did not wish to believe them. A few journalists, among them Arthur Ransome of *Swallows and Amazons* fame, who was heavily biased in favour of the Bolsheviks and was therefore allowed to remain in Russia, did little to penetrate the fog.

Such was the paucity of information about conditions in Soviet Russia that Oliver Harvey of the Russian Department in the Foreign Office in July 1919 wrote a memorandum in the following terms, 'The Bolshevik Government has now held power for over eighteen months. A gentleman who has recently returned from Moscow testified to the general orderliness of that city.'[2] After saying that the Bolshevik forces proved themselves to be efficient soldiers he went on to say, 'It is impossible to account for the stability of the Bolshevik Government by terrorism alone . . . we must admit the fact that the present Russian Government is accepted by the bulk of the Russian people.' The fact that he had to use the testimony of 'a gentleman who has recently returned from Moscow' as a major part of the evidence which led him to such a vitally important conclusion, is graphic testimony of the complete absence of better first-hand information.

It was not that the Allies, and Britain in particular, could not have sent official visitors to Soviet Russia to have a look for themselves. The Soviet leadership would have welcomed any visit of that nature as they welcomed the young American, Bullitt. Lloyd George himself would almost certainly have sent someone there if he had been a free agent, but the Conservative

171

majority in the House of Commons meant that any overt sign of an approach to recognition would have lead to a massive Parliamentary and public upheaval.

As far as the British people as a whole, as opposed to their leaders, were concerned, it cannot be said that the Russian Revolution was an all-absorbing topic of interest at the time. The war against the Germans was physically and in every other way very near to home: Russia was a long way away, a strange people behaving in a very strange, if rather menacing, way, but not directly threatening as were the German and, to a lesser extent, the Austrian hordes. *The Illustrated London News*, that remarkable weekly pictorial and written record of contemporary events and mores, did not even mention the Russian Revolution from 10 November to 8 December 1917. It did, much later on 25 October 1919, have an article about it, 'By one who has just returned from Russia'. It announced:

> *As far as we can judge, Bolshevism owed its inception to three causes. First the obstinacy and bad government of the old regime: secondly, the intrigues on the part of the Germans in Russia and, thirdly, the intrigues and propaganda of the Jews.*

The article then examined these propositions at great length. As far as the Tsar's 'bad government' was concerned:

> *The primary reason . . . was German intrigue: bribery of Ministers and officials and an indirect pro-German influence over the Tsar himself.*

As for German intrigue [presumably through the Tsarina and Rasputin]:

> *The Germans, anticipating a conflict, had permeated Russia economically and most effectively by a system of espionage, bribery and corruption amongst highly placed officials . . . she could not defeat the indomitable Russian soldier in the field and, fair means being out of the question, she decided on foul, and to bring about a revolution in Russia . . . this she did by active revolutionary propaganda . . . and by sending Lenin through*

Germany to Russia no doubt after he had been instructed by the German General Staff in Berlin.

Lastly:

The intrigue and propaganda of the Jews [who] more than any other class have battened on the low wages paid to the Russian workman, and before the Revolution they [the Jews] were most anxious that he should remain in comparative slavery in order that they could fill their pockets. But this was not enough: they desired complete control of Russia in order that they could further increase their gains. It was clear to them that they must first gain ascendancy over what may be termed the intelligent class in Russia . . . the Jews determined to obtain their ascendancy by total extermination of the educated class . . . the instrument that was to carry out this extermination was the so-called proletariat i.e. workmen and peasants. Thus the Jews carried on an active propaganda inciting the proletariat to indulge in a revolution and a massacre of the bourgeoisie.

It is difficult to imagine a more biased and inaccurate description of the causes of the Russian Revolution. Although sent by Germany to Russia, Lenin was not Jewish and would certainly not have obeyed the German General Staff representing a regime which, he was convinced, would collapse to Bolshevism very soon. Whatever else it was and whatever evils permeated its inception, progress and eventual fall, the Russian Revolution was certainly not the result of a German/Jewish conspiracy. Whether or not the writer and those who promoted these ideas believe them to be the truth, this kind of approach to the problems engendered by the Bolshevik Revolution was undoubtedly fairly widespread in Britain.

The result of all this was that it took a very long time for the Allies and Britain to realize the truth that the Bolsheviks were there to stay, that the Red Armies were not a rabble, that the Bolsheviks did have a measure of popular support and that, if they were not to be toppled by intervention on a very large scale, the obvious course was to come to some kind of accommodation

173

with them rather than merely to alienate them without any purpose.

The Peace Conference at Versailles which had been convened for one purpose – the settling of the terms of peace with the Central Powers – found itself trying to deal with another problem – the Russian – and only fitfully at that. There was never any agreement as to the objective to be followed in relation to Russia and the result was the worst of all worlds – a restraint on unilateral decisions by the participants in the faint hope that a joint policy could be arrived at but a complete failure to achieve such a joint policy.

One of the basic problems was that there was no consensus as to what kind of Government should take over. The likelihood must be that if Kolchak or Denikin or Yudenich for that matter, had succeeded, the resulting Government would have been highly autocratic. The fact is that the very qualities which make for successful military leadership militate against the conduct of successful democratic leadership and vice versa, and the transition from the one to the other is fraught with hesitancy and danger.

Another point is that if support is limited to the provision of supplies or money or other non-combatant assistance, as was largely the case in the south and east, the leverage exerted by the supplier of such assistance is small and it is impossible to restrain the excesses which seem inevitably to form part of any civil strife: the behaviour of the Whites in Russia was probably in many ways as bad as that of the Bolsheviks and, certainly, the anti-Jewish pogroms committed by Denikin's troops were appalling. On the other hand if those who intervene actually do the fighting themselves and therefore have considerable leverage, as was the case in North Russia where Ironside became virtual dictator of the Archangel area and, in effect, in the Caucasus where the British actually set up de facto Governments consisting of British army officers, then their opponents can legitimately label them as aggressors against their country and call upon the considerable reserves of patriotic feeling which will certainly be aroused against anyone who attacks an established nation. The Baltic was another matter, where the British Navy seemed to take matters into its own hands. The three Baltic countries did achieve independence, steering a canny course between the tangled web of competing rivalries which surrounded them.

President Wilson virtually opted out of this difficulty by arguing that if the anti-Bolsheviks succeeded in gaining popular goodwill they would win: if they failed to get general support they would lose and would not deserve to win anyway. In a sense, the Allied Intervention to him was concerned with holding the ring so that a fair trial of strength could take place. Like so much else of Wilson's thought this was a highly naïve view of the Russian scene. Much depended on the impact of terror as a weapon and the perceptions of the populace as to which side was in fact likely to win. There was no question of the populace supporting one side or the other because of philosophical agreement with its policies. This was not an election held in the comparative calm of Western democratic procedures, even American democratic procedures. It was a bitter internecine war waged against a background of chaotic starvation-ridden destruction by those who knew that, if they lost, their fate was almost certainly death. The ideological platitudes of small or big-time America did not translate readily to the bloodstained vastness of the Russian state.

All in all, one gets an overwhelming impression of the haphazard nature of the developments covered in the book: Churchill's exuberant disdain for reality in urging further exertions after the total exhaustions of trench warfare; President Wilson's naivety and his vast responsibilities which at times meant that he was too tired to concentrate on the Russian problem; Lloyd George's irrational view of the rights and wrongs of issues depending on who was winning; Kolchak's and Denikin's refusal to abandon hopes of a Greater Russia, vainly defying all attempts at independence on the periphery of the old Russian State; above all, Trotsky's brilliant leadership in the creation of the formidable Red Army out of the remnants of the defeated, totally demoralized, rabble which the Tsarist Army had become.

Out of these, and other, ingredients – none of them inevitable, came the eventual result of Intervention – total victory for the

175

Bolsheviks, total defeat for the interventionists.

Trotsky's creation of the Red Army merits a little further examination. Having negotiated the Brest-Litovsk Treaty he became Commissar for War in mid-March 1918. After the second Revolution, Bolshevik propaganda had been focused on convincing the old Tsarist Army to abandon the war against the Central Powers. The Order No.1 mentioned on page 28 and the subsequent abandonment of capital punishment led, as was intended, to a complete breakdown of military discipline. Faced with what quickly became a Civil War against the Whites on all sides, Trotsky immediately realized, first, that war could only be won by disciplined bodies and, second, that military leadership necessarily involves military experience. The only source of experienced leadership lay in the old Tsarist Army. It was essential, therefore, to get thousands of the old Tsarist officers back into the Red Army. He announced that only 'work, discipline and order will save the Soviet Republic.'[3] He immediately came up against Party ideologues who argued that former Tsarist officers were traitors to the working classes and should not be employed at all, let alone given responsibility. Trotsky insisted that these officers must be employed. For instance, in a letter to a friend on 1 January 1919 he argues that it is necessary to draw in specialists, as he called these ex-Tsarist officers recalled to the Red Army. He goes on:

> In our General Staff Academy there are some Party comrades now studying who have in practice, in bloody experience, conscientiously understood how hard is the stern art of war and who are now working with the greatest attention under the guidance of professors of the old Military School. People who are close to the Academy tell me that the attitude of the pupils to their teachers is not at all determined by political factors, and apparently it is the most conservative of the teachers who is honoured with the most notable marks of attention. These people want to learn. They see beside them others who possess knowledge, and they do not sniff, do not swagger, do not shout tossing their Soviet caps in the air – they learn diligently and conscientiously from the Tsarist Generals because these Generals know what the Communists do not know and what the Communists need to know.[4]

176

Trotsky solved the problems arising from rigid Party dogma by instituting the practice of attaching so-called 'Commissars' to each commander. These functionaries had the task of watching the commanders to whom they were attached to make sure they did not return to their old 'bourgeois' practices and of conducting 'political education' in their units while leaving the commanders to get on with the purely military side of their work. On the face of it this would appear to be an impossible situation for both. But, by and large, it worked. Trotsky himself travelled widely in his personal military train, being utterly ruthless with failures; court martials swiftly followed by executions became almost a matter of routine.

In 1918 no less than 75% of the total of officers in the Red Army had previously been commissioned in the Tsarist Army and by 1919 there were over 30,000 in service.[5] But why did these officers, most of them previously passionately loyal to their Tsar, join an organization which was totally antagonistic to all they had stood for and which had murdered the Tsar and all his family in cold blood at Ekaterinburg? There were a number of comparatively banal answers to this question: to have a job at all in the chaotic conditions of post-Revolutionary Russia; to try to redeem themselves after failure of one sort and another; to use the only skills they had; even, in some cases, because they genuinely believed in the new order of things. However, and this is why Trotsky's achievements have been somewhat laboured in this chapter, one of the reasons was undoubtedly to respond to the attack made on all sides on 'Holy Mother Russia' as the various interventions were seen in many quarters. The onset of civil war was quickly followed by an appeal to Nationalist senti-ment (as indeed occurred after the German invasion in the Second World War). This was one of the most damaging results of Intervention by the anti-Bolsheviks which, in fact, had been accurately forecast by Lloyd George (page 34) and President Wilson (page 38).

Intervention in any civil war on one side will inevitably help the other in so far as the latter can, and will, have a powerful propaganda weapon – join the fight against the foreign invaders. The cynic would argue that if you are going to intervene at all make quite sure that your side wins the military battle, as the Fascists did in Spain.

Furthermore, it is argued by some that the Bolsheviks would not have instituted 'the Terror' after the attempted assassination of Lenin if they had not been able to link the attack on their leader with the Allied Intervention. It is alleged that there was at that stage a very real fear of a Bolshevik collapse aided by the Allied Intervention and that much of the horrific savagery which took place was a very understandable reaction to an anticipated joint attack on all that, as they saw it, the Bolsheviks had created. The Intervention was tangible proof of a foreign determination to overcome the Bolshevik revolution and revert to the status quo in some undetermined form. In fact, of course, to succeed in ousting the Bolsheviks, intervention would have to be massive – and there was no question of the war-weary Allies producing troops on anything like the required scale. Supplies were another matter and an enormous volume of military and other material was sent through Murmansk, Archangel, Vladivostok, Odessa and Novorossisk. Almost all of these items were in fact surplus to requirements as far as the Allies were concerned when the war came to an end.

As all troops of whatever country who have soldiered abroad will know, there is a lighter side to their activities. From shooting duck, fishing, playing rounders with the local children in the north, to race meetings, opera, vast meals with apparently unending vodka and caviare in the south, many of the participating soldiers looked back on their experiences with great pleasure, even nostalgia. There were, of course, as always, extraordinary contrasts. The rollicking, devil-may-care, Russian bonhomie on the one hand and the insouciant killing on the other. As always in war, long periods of intense boredom were followed by short minutes of intense fear, the former in this case predominating.

As far as the other major players in the affair are concerned, the Americans took no real part except in the north where, very reluctantly and directly against the orders of their own President, they fought well, if rather briefly. The French were not really prepared to fight at all when it came to the point and their fleet mutinied in the Black Sea. The Czechs wished to get home, as, after the armistice, did the Germans and Austrians. The Japanese saw the episode merely as an opportunity to grab what land they could; the White Russians, after some initial successes, proved to be a broken reed, their main problem being that they had no agreed political programme to put to the people of Russia as a possible alternative to Bolshevism. There was a total lack of military coordination and, above all, the Whites found themselves up against the brilliant, totally dedicated and ruthless leadership of Trotsky, who, with his interior lines of communication, was able to dash from one trouble spot to another in his train, saving situation after situation with his blend of inspired leadership and the power to bring about instant execution of those who had failed.

There were considerable tensions between the Americans and the British in the north. The Americans hugely resented their subordination to the British Command at every level. For their part, the British were apt, probably totally unfairly, to denigrate the American efforts and their apparent lack of discipline. The French were despised, particularly in the south, where their occupation of Odessa was very short-lived and their fleet mutinied. The French, for their part, probably felt that the Allies had no conception of what they had suffered on the Western Front. The Japanese were disliked and distrusted in equal measure by most, if not all, of the other participants, despite the high hopes which were, at one point, foisted on them by wishful-thinking military staffs.

How did the British soldiers, sailors and airmen react to what they were asked, or indeed ordered, to do? As we have seen, as always there was a good deal of grumbling, in retrospect much of it justified, particularly by those who had been 'volunteered' against their wishes and by the low-category soldiers who were sent straight into action on arrival in the north.

They had to undergo appalling conditions of heat and mosquitoes, followed by extreme cold, both in the north and east. There were, indeed, particularly in the north, signs of incipient mutiny, but these never really came to anything very much. Soldiers are not perfect and no doubt there was a certain amount of loot acquired and other pilfering of one sort or another which would have shocked the statesmen and civil servants sitting in comfort in Versailles and London. But this was as nothing compared to the almost total corruption and dishonesty of many of the White Russian supporters in the south and east. As a whole, except in the north, Transcaspia (where the Indian Army performed valiantly against great odds) and Baku (where Dunsterforce fought well, although vastly outnumbered) the British did little actual fighting. The Baltic episode was an extraordinary event on its own, with little connection to the rest of the Intervention.

By and large, however, the Intervention force was not able to affect the outcome except, as argued above, in so far as it helped Trotsky in his creation of the Red Army. As both Churchill and Bruce Lockhart were to reiterate, the Allies ought either to have intervened on a massive scale or not at all. Half-measures were useless. In fact, of course, massive intervention was quite out of the question as the war-weary West struggled to recover from the most exhausting and lethal war in history.

Nevertheless, as far as the British Servies are concerned, one is left with an overwhelming impression of the quintessential British serviceman with his phlegm, humour, discipline and humanity, carrying on as best he can in often very extraordinary situations without any very clear idea as to why he is there at all.

What lessons are there for us? First, be very careful before you intervene at all in a civil war. Realize that such interventions cannot be limited in time or magnitude of effort. Second, try to find out what is really going on in the country in which you are intending to intervene. Do not be taken in by superficial and biased information, however seductive it might be. Third, make quite sure that the other participants in the intervention have precisely the same aims as you do and that neither you nor they will change their opinion halfway through. Fourth, it is a mistake to embark on military action without overwhelming support at home. Fifth, be sure that you are going to win the military battle and that you have enough available potential reserves to restore the situation if things start to go wrong. Sixth, have a viable political plan ready to put in place after victory with sufficient resources to implement it.

The Intervention in Russia failed in every one of these aspects. At the beginning of the twenty-first century, there is little, if any, sign that Britain and its American Allies have learnt any lessons from this cautionary tale.

APPENDIX A

ORDER

To the Forces of the Northern Region
No. 78
11th December 1918. Archangel.

Yesterday, the 10th December, at 10 o'clock p.m., I was walking near the Lomonosoff School.

From the direction of the Cathedral I heard a disgusting flow of gutter-language. Going nearer, I met two sailors and approaching one of them, I called his attention to the absolute impermissibility of such filthy language in the street.

The second sailor went on, but the one to whom I addressed myself, slovenly declared himself as being drunk, and with a broad gesture he blew his nose on the pavement. Wishing to have a nearer look at this representative of our military power in course of recreation, I directed him to a lighted window. Here I saw that he was without his striped vest. His chest was naked and he had no St George's ribbon on his cap.

I told him that he was improperly dressed and ordered him to follow me to the nearest guard, to whom I would hand him over.

The sailor quickened his pace, rejoined his comrade, and both hurriedly made off. Passing the guard of the Commander-in-Chief I ordered him to stop, but he did not obey. After this, with the help of the British guard, both were arrested.

In the guard-room, the second prisoner began to justify himself, maintaining that he was not to blame. I asked him whether he had his striped vest on. He opened his jacket and I saw a striped vest, clasped at the top with a woman's locket.

I asked myself the question, when will these people realize that they are disgracing the uniform of our native land, by carrying on them women's ornaments?

The names of these sailors were: SAFRONOV, Mihail, from

Trawler T 21, and NEVIADOMSKY, Konstantin, from Trawler T 26.

I request Admiral Vikorst to investigate all this and to act according to law.

How pitiful is all this and how deeply disgusting.

MAROUSHEFFSKÝ

APPENDIX B

ORDER

To the Forces of the Northern Region
No. 100
27th December 1918. Archangel.

Madame Botchkareva arrived from Shenkursk and reported to me on the 26th December. She wore officer's uniform of a Caucasian pattern, with epaulettes. She was accompanied by Lieut. Filipoff, whom she called her adjutant.

Madame Botchkareva offered me her services for work in the organization of the Russian forces.

I do not undertake to estimate the merits of Madame Botchkareva's services in the Russian Army. I consider that the shedding of her blood in the service of her country will be appreciated finally by the Central Government and Russian history.

I only consider it my duty to declare, that within the limits of the northern region, thank God, the time has already come for quiet creative work, and I consider that the summoning of women for military duties, which are not appropriate for their sex, would be a heavy reproach and a disgraceful stain on the whole population of the northern region.

I order that Madame Botchkareva take off her uniform and that Lieut. Filipoff report immediately to the Military Command for registration, to be detailed for duties suitable to his rank and service.

The carrying out of his Order is placed under the supervision of the Town Commandant.

MAROUSHEFFSKY

APPENDIX C

NORTHERN RUSSIA'S WELCOME
Governor General Miller's Tribute to Britons

In the reign of Queen Elizabeth daring sailors and traders from England arrived in Archangel, which was then part of the dominions of the Muscovite Tsar, John the Terrible. Here, on the banks of the Dvina, Englishmen and Russians met for the first time.

Archangel received the strangers with courtesy, and they were regarded by the Terrible Tsar with favour. He invited them to visit him in Ancient Moscow, where he received them cordially and granted them, before they left his presence, a Trading Charter which assisted the relations between the two countries.

Much time has passed since. England and Russia, guided by their statesmen, have pursued their own courses in history, more than once passing through historical crises which shook Europe – sometimes fighting shoulder to shoulder against a common enemy and sometimes meeting as opponents. And, as the political lives of our countries followed their own courses, so did the lives of our peoples.

In Ancient Moscow, the heart of Russia, in St Petersburg, the young and splendid Russian Capital, and in other parts of the immense Russian State, British Colonies appeared and flourished. The British brought us their knowledge, and sent to Russia the merchandise she needed.

On the field of battle and in peaceful work among our people, Englishmen, from time immemorial, have been known to us as people of undaunted courage, of practical working ability, always unswerving in their aims and unwaveringly honest in their dealings. Russians came to value the word of an Englishman higher than any written bond. The English word "Gentleman" was adopted into the Russian language, and in every Englishman, before all else, we always expect to see a gentleman.

Three and a half centuries passed, and again the British landed on the banks of the Dvina, where their help was needed. Russia was under the heel of the Bolshevik – the Bolshevik who, in the middle of the great war, treacherously signed the Brest-Litovsk Treaty, committed the most unheard-of crimes in Russia (one of their victims was Captain Cromie of the British Navy), threw hundreds of innocent sons of Britain into prison, and finally aroused the indignation of the British Government which, a year ago, sent troops to the distant North of Russia – to Murman and Archangel.

These troops formed the outpost, under the protection of which began the creation of the Russian Army for the struggle for the deliverance of Russia from the despotic power of the one-time German agents, the traitorous Bolsheviks.

These tyrants and outcasts – mostly aliens – stained with the guilt of every kind of crime, helped by Germans and supported by Lettish and Chinese mercenaries, have, by deception force and terror, enslaved a portion of the simple and ignorant Russian people.

Now we have witnessed the arrival of further British troops. These soldiers volunteered to strengthen the "outpost" in order to help Russia to free herself from the yoke of the Bolshevik.

Welcome! Gallant British Soldiers, hastening in disinterested and self-sacrificing aid in the struggle for the deliverance of Russia from the miscreants under whose yoke the majority of the Russian people groan.

Long live Great Britain, who helps us to re-build our Mother Country on a basis of Right and Justice.

WELCOME! BRITAIN's Outpost.

(Signed) E Miller

GOVERNOR GENERAL NORTH RUSSIA

APPENDIX D

Why don't you return home?

To the American and British Soldiers

Comrades.

The war is over, why are you not returning home? The people in England and America went nearly mad with joy when the long hoped for peace at last arrived. But why is there no peace for you, and for us? President Wilson and his colleagues are in Europe, the other Allied governments have also appointed their delegates, and soon the Peace Conference will assemble. But in the meantime you are still condemned to fight and die, and war with all its horrors is raging in Russia.

For many long, weary agonising months, perhaps years your old folks, you (sic) wives, your little ones have been overwhelmed with anxiety about you. Now in their innocence their anxiety has been turned into joyful expectation of your return. Can you not picture them; – every knock, every footstep they here (sic) makes their hearts leap in the belief that it is someone bringing tidings of your homecoming. But your dear ones will wait in vain; your masters continue to drive you through the valley of death, and you do not know, but that your bodies may rot in the mud and blood of the battlefield. Don't you want to mingle with your loved ones again?

The war is over. Why don't you go home?

For over four years your governments have kept you at war, and have condemned millions of your fellow citizens to death, and millions more to a fate worse than death. You made these fearful sacrafices (sic) for what you were led to believe to be the defence of Europe against the domination of the Kaiser, and once and for all to relieve the world from the crushing burden of armaments; from the menace of Prussian militarism.

Well, this menace is now removed. Prussian militarism is crushed. The Kaiser is a fugitive. The German workers have risen in revolt and have delivered a death blow to the power of the reactionary Junker class.

Why then are you still fighting? Above all why are you in Russia?

The help of the Allied Governments against Germany was never desired by Russia. It is now quite unnecessary. It was never intended that the Allied troops in Russia were to fighta (sic) Germans. This is perfectly obvious now since the war with Germany is apparently over, and yet the war against the Russian people still continues. Why? The reason is not far to seek.

The workers and peasants in Russia have done what your rulers fear you will do, they have swept the whole-class of parasites, courtiers, landlords, and capitalists out of power, and have taken posession (sic) of the land and the means of production for the use of the whole people. The Russian people refuse to be the slaves of an idle class any longer. They are constructing a new order of society in which the products of labour will go to those who work. The spirit which animates the Russian people has spread westward, and now the Austrian, Hungarian, and German people have overthrown their rules (sic) are rapidly travelling along the same lines as the workers of Russia. It is the awakening of the real democracy that we are witnessing to-day: The common workers in field, factory, and mine are asserting their right and power to rule, and be masters of their own destiny.

Your masters see that the spirit of revolt is spreading to your countries. In both England and America the ideas of Bolshevism is making rapid headway. Great Labour demonstrations frequently take place at which the workers demand that the means of wealth production shall be taken over by the workers. At these meetings strong protests are expressed against the invasion of Russia. Your masters know that the source and centre of the revolutionary World movement is Russia, and they are determined therefore to crush it out, and remove the menace to their power. That is why you are here. That is why your masters will not permit you to rejoin your loved ones who are eagerly looking forward to your return.

You see that the war has now been converted into a gigantic conflict between Labour and Capital. It is a conflict between Progress and Reaction. A conflict between those who are inaugurating a new era of social and economic liberty for the toiling masses, and those who decire (sic) to retain the present sordid commercial system, with its sweating, poverty, and war. And you who obey the orders of your governments are fighting to maintain the old order, you are fighting on the side of Reaction against the forces of Labour and Progress.

Is this worth dying for? Do you really desire to bleed and die in order that capitalism may continue. Say no?

Form Soldier's Councils in each regiment, and demand of your government, demand of your officers to be sent home. Refuse to shoot your fellow workers in Russia. Refuse to crush-our (sic) **Workers Revolution.**

The Group of English-speaking Communists.

APPENDIX E

1. A General Strike has taken place in Baku in defiance of my proclamation issued on my arrival here on November 17th 1918.

2. This strike is a severe hardship to the workmen and inhabitants of the town.

3. I appeal to the moderate men of all parties to use their influence to bring to an end this interference with their peaceful lives.

4. So long as the strike continues I am prevented from taking any action to release those who have been arrested under Martial Law for the preservation of public order.

5. Representations have been made to me by General Bicherakov, to Russia's National Council and others to release certain of those arrested. At General Bicherakov's representation I have ordered one man to be released. When the strike is over I shall favourably consider other cases for release.

6. It must be clearly understood therefore that those now on strike are directly responsible for preventing any act of clemency of my part.

7. It is therefore the duty of all to work for the immediate cessation of the strike.

So long as it is possible I shall continue to arrange for the feeding of the people but the Railways and Shipping must resume work to enable this to be done.

(signed) W.M. THOMSON
Major-General
Military Governor, BAKU

(In pencil on the top of this was written 'May be communicated to Officers and OR'. [other ranks])

APPENDIX F

This is an exact copy of the propaganda which the Bolsheviks gave to the British sailors.

<u>English Sailors!</u> What base influence forces you to fire at the Revolutionary Russian Army? Don't you see that you fire at your brothers and friends. We are just the same working people as you.

We Russian workmen and peasants are wrestling against reactionaries who want to take away from us lands and factories and give them back to capitalists and landlords.

They want to restore again the power of the capitalists instead of the power of the working people as it is now in the Soviet Russia. General Denikin's Army against which we are fighting is composed of officers who are the sons of rich merchants and landlords.

The Red Army is an army of workmen and peasants who have voluntarily joined the ranks to protect the Revolution.

<u>English Sailors!</u> You are also working people, all of you have neither castles nor factories. We have no enmity with you, just the opposite, we look upon you as brothers. Then why do you fire at us? They are afraid that if our Communistic country will be strengthened the working people of other countries including the English working class, will follow our example. Also the feeling of solidarity forces them to help Russian capitalists and reactionaries who pray for help. This is why, this is for what reasons your Government keeps you in the Black Sea far from your home and families.

Do you know why your Commanders don't allow you to visit the sea shore in Theodosia? Because they are afraid lest you should as soon as you know the truth demand to stop immediately the bombarding of our positions. So it was in Sebastapol where the French sailors after having visited several times the shore told Admiral Amette that they want to be sent immediately home. More than that they organized a demonstration with Red flags and also presented us a Red flag. They told us that they like us and sympathise with us. After that their Squadron immediately left the Black Sea.

Even the French officers and among them Admiral Amette, said that they are against fighting with the Red Army.

Now the French sailors are at home.

What are you here for? Return home. Don't interfere with our affairs. Don't prevent the Russian workmen and peasants from building their own life.

Have you nothing to do at home?

Aren't your wives and children waiting for you? Capitalists have profited millions on military prohibitions, now they want to exploit the Russian people and take from them the remains which the Germans had no time to rob.

Down with the capitalistic Governments of all countries.

Long live the fraternity of nations.

Long live the revolutionary British sailor.

Down with the War.

The Movable Printing Office of the Political Department of the Crimean Red Army.

This is an exact copy.

Signed P.J.S.

APPENDIX G

Officers and soldiers of the most powerfull
Navy of Great Britain!

Just a month ago we stopped with your friendly help the advancing of the bolcheviks on the peninsula of Kertch.

During our mutual military labour were difinitly strengthened the fraternal relations between the russian army and the navy of Great Britain. Now we have been persuaded not only by words but by facts, that Great Britain wants to help us quite sincerily and inflexibily and to save the great Russia from the bloody civil war.

Neither the intrigues of the bolcheviks, nor the natural tired state after the long war could shake you and you stay like before on the guard of humanity and international justice.

Children of the great country, which is the cradle of political freedom and example of high civism!

Take our warmest thanks for your powerfull help. which is coming just at time in our heavy war with the corruptors of our fatherland the bolcheviks-the worlds peril!

The new Russia will never forget your help.

Commander of the Voluntary Army of the Crimy and Azoff.
General-Lieutenant **Borovsky.**

12-25 May 1919.

NOTES

Chapter 1

1.   Charles Hudson had a highly distinguished record in the First World War. He had won the Victoria Cross, the Distinguished Service Order and Bar, the Military Cross, the French Croix de Guerre and the Italian Silver Al Valore Militare. Aged twenty-six, he had commanded the Second Battalion of the Sherwood Foresters during the final battles in France and the advance to Germany. Shortly after the war ended he became ill and was sent on sick leave for three months. He was told, when he returned to his battalion, that since some officers senior to him were joining from jobs elsewhere he would have to relinquish his command and would be lucky if he became second in command of a company with the rank of Captain. He had heard that there were 'several British forces spread around the borders of Bolshevik Russia, supporting the White Russians, and I was curious to know what was going on, both in the military and political sense.' He asked to be posted to one of these forces, but this was refused. He heard that boats for North Russia sailed from Harwich so he went there and hitched a lift to Murmansk on an American boat. Having arrived there, after an abortive attempt to reach Archangel by dog sleigh, by bribing the Captain with whisky, he managed to board a Russian ice-cutter which was making the first attempt, in spring 1919, to get through to Archangel. In spite of its drunken Captain the vessel succeeded in reaching Archangel and Hudson went to see General Ironside, the formidable Commander-in-Chief, who gave him the job of Brigade Major to Brigadier General Turner, who was in command of the railway front. Ironside also promised to send a telegram to the War Office informing them that Hudson was gainfully employed and had not deserted. All the references to Hudson in this and subsequent passages come either from his journal, privately published under the title *Two Lives 1892–1992* or from personal talks with his son – the author of this book.

2.   Interview with author on 5 July 1983
3.   Interview with author on 4 March 1982
4.   Blacker, *On Secret Patrol in High Asia*, Murray, pages 8, 17, 28,
     30, 31
5.   Interview with author on 5 July 1983
6.   Interview with author on 5 July 1983

Chapter 2

1.   Charles Hudson's remarks to author
2.   The modern, Western, calendar will be used throughout
3.   Louis de Robien, *The Diary of a Diplomat in Russia in
     1917–1918*, Michael Joseph, page 257
4.   de Robien, op cit, pages 159, 160, 161 and 274
5.   Gilbert, *Winston S. Churchill*, Volume 4, page 230
6.   Gilbert, op cit, page 22
7.   This problem was eventually solved under heavy pressure from
     the Allies by the acceptance of Kolchak's authority by all three
     major White leaders – Tchaikovsky and, later, Miller in the north
     and Denikin in the south, although Kolchak was never fully
     recognized by the Allies because of his refusal, except in the cases
     of Poland and Finland, to accept full independence of those
     peripheral states which were demanding it.
8.   The origin, purpose and course of the Bullitt Mission remains
     somewhat obscure. The episode is examined in detail in Gregor
     Dallas's book *1918*, Murray, pages 370-377. What is beyond
     doubt is that Bullitt was young, rich, clever and determined to
     move American policy towards accommodation with the
     Bolsheviks, whom he admired.

Chapter Three

1.   Ullman, *Intervention and the War*, volume 1, Princeton
     University Press, page 113
2.   Maynard, *The Murmansk Venture*, Hodder & Stoughton, page
     28. Maynard also had the services of the 'Karelian Regiment' at
     Kem, formed by the people of Karelia. They wished passionately
     for independence, hating the Russians and the Finns equally.
     They were commanded by a Colonel Woods, who forwarded a
     petition to Maynard asking King George to take them on as a

Protectorate. This was far too difficult for Whitehall. They became disaffected and were disbanded. Colonel Woods's diary, Imperial War Museum. (IWM)

3.   Drage, Diary IWM
4.   Rhodes, *The Anglo-American WinterWar with Russia 1918/19*, Greenwood Press, page 27
5.   Watson, Diary IWM
6.   Bracher, Diary IWM
7.   Gilbert, *Churchill*, volume 4, 1916-22, page 257
8.   Rhodes, op cit, page 26
9.   Ullman, op cit, volume 1, page 241
10. Maynard, op cit, page 23
11. Hirst, Diary IWM
12. Thompson, Diary IWM
13. Gawthorpe, Diary IWM
14. Tyler, Diary IWM
15. Rhodes, op cit, page 33
16. Rhodes, op cit, page 35
17. Ullman, op cit, page 244
18. Roeber, Diary IWM
19. Rhodes, op cit, page 69, letter from Herman Sheiter to Emil Haller
20. Rhodes, op cit, page 61
21. Gilmore, Diary IWM
22. Ironside, *Archangel 1918/19*, Constable, page 31
23. Ullman, op cit, page 237
24. Ullman, op cit, page 252
25. Ullman, op cit, page 256
26. Information from Charles Hudson
27. Watson, Diary IWM
28. Ironside, op cit, page 51
29. Halliday, *The Ignorant Armies*, Weidenfeld & Nicolson, page 4
30. Halliday, ibid, page 6
31. Wilson, Diary IWM
32. Ironside, op cit, page 78
33. e.g. Charles Hudson's Journal
34. Hirst, Diary IWM
35. Max Arthur, *The True Glory, the Royal Navy 1914–1939*, Hodder and Stoughton, pages 169–183
36. Max Arthur, ibid, page 182

37. Ullman, *Britain and the Russian Civil War*, volume 2, letter from Churchill to Lloyd George, page 178
38. Pond, Diary IWM
39. *Hampshire Regimental History*, Part 2, page 43
40. Rhodes, op cit, page 106
41. General Richardson's report to the Adjutant General of the Army 27 July 1919, quoted in Rhodes, op cit, page 107
42. Charles Hudson in his journal notes that the truth was that the Hampshire Regiment Commanding Officer had lost his nerve. He turned white and trembled when a few shells landed some way off
43. Wilson, Diary IWM
44. Roupell, Diary IWM
45. Thompson, Diary IWM
46. Gawthorpe, Diary IWM
47. Ironside, op cit, page 68
48. Pond, Diary IWM
49. Gas was used by the British on both fronts – see Pond's remarks here, Rhodes, op cit, page 116-7 and Charles Hudson's Journal. When Churchill was asked about this in the House of Commons he agreed that gas had been used but said that the Bolsheviks had also used it. On the face of it this seems unlikely and the author has been unable to find any evidence to that effect.
50. Ironside, op cit, page 180
51. Ullman, op cit, volume 2, page 198
52. Bowen, Diary, IWM
53. Max Arthur, op cit, pages 137/8

Chapter Four

1. Hampshire Regiment Archives
2. Farmborough, *Nurse at the Russian Front 1914–18*, Constable, page 402
3. Howgreave Graham, an officer of the 1st/9th battalion Hampshire Regiment kept a diary quoted in Fleming's *The fate of Admiral Kolchak*, Hart-Davis, page 92
4. Victor Cazalet, ADC to General Knox – Diary quoted in Fleming, op cit, page 92
5. Reardon, Diary IWM

6. Much of what follows is taken from *With the Diehards in Siberia* by Colonel John Ward, CB, CMG, MP
7. Ward, op cit, page 51
8. Reardon, Diary IWM
9. Ullman, op cit, Volume 1, page 276
10. Fleming, op cit, page 52
11. Ward, op cit, page 126
12. Ullman, op cit, Volume 1, page 279
13. Hampshire Regiment Territorial War Record and *Journal of the Hampshire Regiment*
14. Horrocks, *A Full Life*, Collins, page 36
15. Horrocks, op cit, page 45
16. Jupe, Hampshire Regiment Archive
17. Fleming, op cit, page 126
18. Fleming, op cit, page 219
19. Jupe, Hampshire Regiment Archive
20. Ivens, Diary IWM
21. Horrocks, op cit, page 59
22. *The Lancashire Lad*, March and June 1958
23. Ivens, Diary IWM

Chapter 5

1. Ullman, *Intervention and the War*, Volume 1, Princeton, page 304
2. Ullman, ibid, page 305
3. Major-General L.C. Dunsterville, *Adventures of Dunsterforce*, Arnold, and lecture to the Central Asian Society, 16 December 1920.
    Major-General Malleson, lecture to the Central Asian Society, 24 January 1922.
    Sir George McCartney, lecture to the Central Asian Society, 11 June 1919.
4. Perrett and Lord, *The Czar's British Squadron*, Kimber
5. Dunsterville, op cit, page 219
6. Leslie Missen, interview with author 21 September 1982
7. Captain Norris, lecture to the Central Asian Society, 12 April 1923
8. Dunsterville, op cit, page 286
9. Ullman, op cit, page 310

10. Interview with author, 21 September 1982
11. Franks, Diary IWM
12 Material from documents of Captain Pertwee, IWM
13. Bowhill, Diary IWM
14 Snow, Letter IWM
15. Bilney, Papers IWM
16. Grundy, Material IWM
17. Captain Norris, lecture to the Central Asian Society, 12 April 1923
18. Lecture cited above
19. C.H. Ellis, *The Transcaspian Episode*, Hutchinson, page 22. Ellis himself was one of the Russian and Persian speaking officers.
20. Ellis, ibid, page 79
21. Malleson, lecture cited above
22. Bailey, *Mission to Tashkent*, Jonathan Cape, page 41
23. Blacker, *On Secret Patrol in High Asia*, Murray
24. Bailey, op cit, page 26
25. Blacker, op cit
26. Bailey, op cit, page 32
27. McCartney, lecture cited above
28. Bailey, op cit, page 120

Chapter Six

1. Stell documents in IWM, Misc 204, Item 2972
2. Ullman, *Britain and the Russian Civil War*, Vol 2, Princeton University, page 67, quoted from the Minutes of the Eastern Committee. Much of what follows comes from the same book.
3. The relationship between Balfour and Curzon was most bizarre. In early 1919 Lloyd George decided to maintain his War Cabinet so that the members of it could help him in the Paris peace negotiations. Balfour remained Foreign Secretary, while Curzon, as Lord President of the Council, took charge of the Foreign Office in London. This was an impossible situation, particularly since the personalities of Balfour and Curzon were so very different – both brilliant intellectually, but Balfour indolent to a degree, Curzon hard working to a fault. The position could not be maintained indefinitely and in October 1919 Curzon eventually became Foreign Secretary.

He set out his view of Balfour in a note he wrote in November 1922 (quoted in *Curzon*, David Gilmore, Murray, page 503):

His charm of manner, his extraordinary intellectual distinction, his seeming indifference to petty matters, his power of dialectic, his long and honourable career of public service, blinded all but those who knew from the inside to the lamentable ignorance, indifference and the levity of his regime. He never studied his papers; he never knew the facts; at the Cabinet he had seldom read the morning's Foreign Office telegrams; he never got up a case; he never looked ahead. He trusted to his unequalled powers of improvisation to take him through any trouble and enable him to leap lightly from one crisis to another.

4. Ullman, Volume 2, page 84
5. Baker, papers, IWM
6. Page, papers, IWM. The author rode in a mule race in Palestine in 1946. The difficulty was in steering. A blow with a stick on the side of the head had to suffice.
7. Page, ibid
8. Beresford Ash, Journal, IWM
9. Bechhofer, In *Denikin's Russia*, Collins, pages 18-38
10. Max Arthur, *The Royal Navy 1914–39, The True Glory*, Hodder and Stoughton, pages 161–168
11. Le Brun, letters, IWM

Chapter Seven

1. Luckett, *The White Generals*, Routledge and Kegan Paul, page 100
2. Ullman, *Intervention in the War*, Volume 1, Princeton University, page 56
3. Jackson, *At War with the Bolsheviks*, Stacey, page 175
4. Ullman, *Britain and the Russian Civil War*, Volume 2, page 60
5. Ullman, op cit, page 212
6. Bostock, Diary IWM
7. Ullman, op cit, Volume 2, page 213
8. Farmer, Diary IWM
9. Churchill, *The World Crisis, The Aftermath*, Thornton Butterworth, page 255
10. Much of what follows comes from Dobson and Miller, *The Day*

We Almost Bombed Moscow, Hodder and Stoughton and from the archives of the Tank Museum at Bovingdon, Dorset

11. Churchill, op cit, page 232
12. Churchill, op cit, page 234
13. Lancaster, Diary IWM
14. C.E. Bechhofer, *In Denikin's Russia*, Collins, page 121
15. McPherson, letter, IWM
16. Wood, journal, IWM
17. Wyld, diary IWM
18. Swinley, journal, IWM
19. Durnford, journal, IWM
20. Shrubsole, letter, IWM
21. Ullman, *The Anglo-Soviet Accord*, Princeton University, page 31

Chapter Eight

1. Lieven, *The Baltic Revolution*, Yale University Press, page 59
2. Nicolson, *Alex*, Weidenfeld and Nicolson, 1973, page 50
3. Hunter, Diary IWM
4. Foreign Office Memorandum respecting the situation in the South Baltic States quoted in Ullman, *Britain and the Russian Civil War*, Princeton University, 1968, page 256
5. Nicolson, op cit, page 58
6. Dukes, *The Story of ST 25*, Cassell, page 311
7. Born in 1871, Cowan was a remarkable man. Having joined the navy he managed to get himself involved in the battle of Omdurman in 1898 and in the South African War. He took part in the battle of Jutland and, as described here, commanded the British fleet in the Baltic in 1919 (for which he was made a Baronet). In the Second World War, aged seventy, he was attached to the Commandos in the Middle East where he took part in actions at Bardia and Tobruk. He then joined the 18th King Edward VIIs own Indian Cavalry Regiment as some kind of liaison officer and, at the Battle of Bir Hakeim, having emptied his revolver at an Italian armoured car, he was eventually captured, aged seventy-one, and evacuated to Italy. Nine months later, because of his age, he was exchanged for an Italian general and arrived back in England. He then managed to get himself back to Italy where he rejoined the Commandos and fought with them in the Dalmatian Islands, gaining a bar to the Distinguished

Service Order he had originally won forty-three years before in South Africa. He was also made Honorary Colonel of the Indian Cavalry Regiment in which he had served in North Africa, surely a unique honour for a naval officer. In his youth, on 10 September 1900 he had ridden in all seven horse races at a meeting held by the Field Force, South Africa, winning one and coming second and third in two others (information from Captain Lionel Dawson, RN, *Sound of the Guns*, Oxford Pen in Hand, 1949).

8. Brewerton, Diary, IWM
9. Agar's exploits have been taken from his book – *Baltic Episode*, Hodder and Stoughton, 1963
10. McCall, Diary, IWM
11. Ullman, op cit, page 274 and Geoffrey Bennett, *Cowan's War*, Collins, Appendix
12. Waymouth, Diary IWM
13. Hampsheir, Diary IWM
14. Ullman, op cit, page 283
15. These tanks had originally been intended for Murmansk but were diverted to the North Western Army, their crews to act as instructors. However, as had occurred with Denikin's Army, they soon became actively engaged themselves. They fought well but, due to problems of maintenance and supply, they were only able to field three tanks at a time. They reached Gatchina, only twenty-two miles from Petrograd, on 15 October 1919, but had to withdraw and return to Britain in November 1919.

Chapter Nine

1. Peter Fleming, *The Fate of Admiral Kolchak*, Hart Davis, page 151
2. Ullman, *Britain and the Russian Civil War*, Princeton University Press, page 176
3. Bruce Lincoln, *Red Victory*, Simon and Schuster, page 173
4. Leon Trotsky, *Military Writings*, Merit Publishers, page 151
5. Luckett, *The White Generals*, Routledge and Kegan Paul, page 237

SELECT BIBLIOGRAPHY

Agar, *Baltic Episode*, Hodder and Stoughton
Arthur, *The Royal Navy, 1914–1939*, Hodder and Stoughton
Bennett, *Cowan's War*, Collins
Bailey, *Mission to Tashkent*, Jonathan Cape
Bechhofer, *In Denikin's Russia*, Collins
Blacker, *On Secret Patrol in High Asia*, Murray
Central Asian Society Journal, Lectures by Dunsterville, Malleson, McCartney, Norris
Churchill, *The World Crisis, The Aftermath*, Thornton Butterworth
Crown Copyright, *The Russian Revolution, 1917*
Dawson, *Sound of the Guns*, Oxford Pen-in-Hand
De Robien, *The Story of a Diplomat in Russia 1917–18*, Michael Joseph
Dobson and Miller, *The Day We Almost Bombed Moscow*, Hodder and Stoughton
Dotsenko, *The Struggle for Democracy in Siberia 1917–20*, Hoover Institution Press
Dukes, *The Story of ST25*, Cassell
Ellis, *The Transcaspian Episode 1918–19*, Hutchinson
Farmborough, *Nurse at the Russian Front 1914–18*, Constable
Fleming, *The Fate of Admiral Kolchak*, Hart-Davis
Gilbert, *Churchill*, Volume 4
Gilmore, *Curzon*, Murray
Halliday, *The Ignorant Armies*, Weidenfeld and Nicolson
Hankey, *The Supreme Control at the Paris Peace Conference 1919*, Allen and Unwin
Hopkirk, *On Secret Service East of Constantinople*, Stacey
Ironside, *Archangel 1918–19*, Constable
Kennan, *Decision to Intervene*, Faber and Faber
Kettle, *The Allies and the Russian Collapse*, Andre Deutsch
Lieven, *The Baltic Revolution*, Yale University Press
Lincoln, *Red Victory*, Da Capa Press
Lockhart, *Memoirs of a British Agent*, MacMillan
Luckett, *The White Generals*, Routledge and Kegan Paul
Macmillan, *Peacemakers*, Murray

Mawdsley, *The Russian Civil War*, Allen and Unwin

Maynard, *The Murmansk Venture*, Hodder and Stoughton

Nicolson, *Alex*, Hodder and Stoughton

Owen, *Tempestuous Journey, Lloyd George His Life and Times*, Hutchinson

Perrott and Lord, *The Czar's British Squadron*, Penguin

Rhodes, *The Anglo/American Winter War with Russia 1918–19*, Greenwood Press

Shuckman, *The Russian Revolution*, Sutton

Teague-Jones, *The Spy Who Disappeared*, Gollanz

Thompson, *Revolutionary Russia 1917*, MacMillan

Trotsky, *Military Writings*, Merit Publishers

Ullman, *Intervention and the War*, Volume 1, Princeton University Press

Ullman, *Britain and the Russian Civil War*, Volume 2, Princeton University Press

Ullman, *The Anglo-Soviet Accord*, Volume 3, Princeton University Press

Ward, *With the Diehards in Siberia*, Cassell

INDEX